Housegroups

Housegroups

The leaders' survival guide

editors Ian Coffey and
Stephen Gaukroger

Crossway Books
Leicester

CROSSWAY BOOKS
38 De Montfort Street, Leicester LE1 7GP, England

First published 1996

British Library Cataloguing in Publication Data
A catalogue record for this book is available from the British Library.

ISBN 1-85684-148-0

Set in Franklin Gothic

Typeset in Great Britain by Textype Typesetters, Cambridge

Printed in Great Britain by Clays Ltd, St Ives plc

CONTENTS

About the editors

Ian Coffey is Senior Minister at Mutley Baptist Church in Plymouth. He served as Field Director for the Evangelical Alliance of the UK and has travelled extensively as Bible teacher and evangelist. As a leader in the local church he is firmly committed to the small-group concept for Bible study, evangelism, fellowship and prayer. He is the author of several books.

Ian is married to Ruth and they have four sons. When he is allowed to have time off he enjoys golf, sailing and reading.

Stephen Gaukroger is Minister of Gold Hill Baptist Church in Buckinghamshire. He was President of the Baptist Union of Great Britain from 1994 to 1995 and is Chairman of the European Board of the Luis Palau Evangelistic Association. A prolific author, his books include *It makes sense*, *Why bother with mission?* and a three-volume popular series *Growing with John's Gospel*.

Stephen is married to Janet who is very involved with work among the under fives and family worship. They have three young children.

Ian and Stephen together act as series editors for the *Crossway Bible Guides*. They had the original idea for this book, believing that housegroup leaders are often the unsung heroes of local church life!

Introduction

They are dedicated and usually very busy people with many demands on their time.

They get a great deal of satisfaction in seeing others grow in faith.

They enjoy having people in their homes and get a buzz from teaching the Bible and seeing Christians gripped by its message.

They are often overlooked in the hustle and bustle of local church life and it doesn't usually bother them a great deal.

They are people who have a special part to play in the purposes of God.

If that description fits you, the chances are you are now, have been in the past, or one day will be – a housegroup leader.

We hope you noticed that we didn't say you were a super-spiritual giant who rises each day at 4 a.m. to pray and reads Scripture only in the original Hebrew or Greek. That may be the picture an average housegroup member has of you, but we know different!

The truth is, you are an ordinary Christian with the same pressures, joys, temptations and encouragements that any of us face. There are times when you find it tough following Jesus and leading a housegroup. There are evenings when your heart sinks as the living-room fills up. There are days when you want to give up, but your sense of duty always gets you to change your mind before you write the resignation letter.

How come we seem to know so much about *you*?

Because the two of us are senior pastors of busy churches where people like *you* are the backbone of what goes on. We have the privilege (and challenge!) of teaching the Word of God to hundreds of people Sunday by Sunday and we know the demands that makes on us. But we also recognize that running a home, a job and a housegroup makes equally heavy demands. People like *you* are special.

Perhaps that will help you to understand why this book has been written. We have been involved for the past few years as Series Editors for the *Crossway Bible Guides*. Together with our colleagues, Stephen Dray, who teaches at Moorlands College and Stephen Motyer who teaches at London Bible College, we have been steadily working with various authors to produce a series of Bible Commentaries written in down-to-earth language. They aim to explain the meaning of the text of Scripture and apply it for Christians living in today's world. We have tried to keep in our minds people like you, who have the responsibility of leading a small group of people who meet regularly to study the Bible.

We have used as authors, gifted people who are in the business of teaching the Bible to others and are doing it well. It has been encouraging to learn of the way in which *Crossway Bible Guides* have found an acceptance in all sorts of churches across the UK as well as further afield in the USA and other parts of the world.

It was through working together on the *Crossway Bible Guides* that we saw the need for a resource book for housegroup leaders, a sort of *Yellow Pages* directory that would cover some of the main things a housegroup leader will face in leading a group over a period of a few years.

We know from our experience in our own local congregations some of the questions housegroup leaders ask:

- How can I develop my skills as a leader?
- Are there ways in which worship and prayer can be developed in the group?
- How can I get some people to contribute more – and others to talk less?
- Can you use a housegroup for outreach?

- How can we move to a deeper level of fellowship?
- How does my housegroup fit into the wider work of God in my local church?
- How can I make my own teaching of the Bible more creative and helpful to the members of the group?

With these and other questions in mind, we looked around to find people who have hands-on experience of leading small groups. We gave them a specific issue and asked them to give us the benefit of their experiences over the years. And what you have in front of you now are their insights which they are willing to pass on. So here it is; a complete housegroup leaders' survival guide – well, as complete as it can be! At least it's an honest attempt to get you started, give you some ideas that work and a few words of encouragement along the way.

Probably there are twenty or so other things that we could have tackled. But we will have to deal with those in another book. Who knows, your housegroup could have become such a success story that you will be writing one of the chapters!

One last thing. A lesson we are continually learning in Christian ministry we would like to pass on to you. Give 101% of heart, enthusiasm and dedication. That will have a bigger impact on your group than even the most sparkling Bible study. Enjoy reading!

Ian Coffey
Stephen Gaukroger

Stephen Dray is a lecturer and pastoral tutor at Moorlands College and a visiting lecturer at the Central European Bible Institute at Budapest. At home he is husband to schoolteacher Anne, father to three children and deacon to Winton Baptist Church, Bournemouth. He is one of the editors of the Crossway Bible Guides.

He describes himself as a keen reader, especially of whodunnits and thrillers, a sports watcher and occasional club cricketer.

What's the point of housegroups?

Stephen Dray

Housegroups in the Bible?

It's a funny thing; you and I can read and re-read the Bible and (to use a phrase used by C. S. Lewis in a different context) see fern seed at a distance while we fail to see the elephant standing right in front of us. Suddenly, we are brought face to face with something that we had never seen before . . . and then discover the same thing everywhere we look!

The church can experience this too. Sometimes we seem to have spotted the most obscure things in the Scriptures but failed to notice the obvious. This is surely so in the case of housegroups. Not that the word occurs in the Bible; but then neither does the term 'Trinity'. However, just as when we read the Scriptures the fact of God's threeness in oneness underlies so much of what we read, the same is true of 'housegroups'. They are implied but not described.

The Old Testament

The spiritual life of the people of God was entrusted to the leaders of ancient Israel. Priests and prophets were called upon by God to instruct the people in his ways; the king was expected to show an example of godly living and the wise men and women offered advice for life which was rooted in the fear of the Lord.

Yet alongside this, there was the responsibility of the extended family to ensure that one generation passed on to the next a knowledge of God and his ways (see, for example, Deuteronomy 6:1–7).

There are those today who suggest that we should 'reactivate' the extended family in the modern world. Certainly the Old Testament recognized that the smaller and more intimate group was vital in supplementing the ministry of the nation's leaders and providing a context in which the people of God could grow to full maturity.

So there you have it; 'housegroups' in the Old Testament!

The New Testament

We have scarcely opened the New Testament before we discover that Jesus started a 'housegroup'; for, in many respects, that is exactly what the disciples were. Expertly led by Jesus (have you considered him as a model for a housegroup leader?) the disciples were taught and equipped for service through the teaching and example of the master.

But what about elsewhere in the New Testament? Increasingly, as people set aside the traditional model of 'church' and recognize that the early disciples met neither in lofty cathedrals nor tin tabernacles, it becomes apparent that the early church frequently met as 'housegroups'. The direct evidence is scanty but compelling. While Paul could, for example, speak of 'the church in Corinth' or 'the church in Rome', it becomes apparent that the one in each city seems to have been composed of a number of different 'cells' or 'housegroups'; some of which are named (Romans 16:3–5; Colossians 4:15; Philemon 2; in each of these cases 'church' seems to refer to a group within the wider 'church' in the city).

We can only speculate as to what took place in these gatherings. However, the New Testament is very clear as to the purpose of 'church', and it would seem likely that in groups people were nourished through mutually sharing in prayer and in the instruction of the Christian faith. It seems probable that they functioned as the 'sharp-end' of the church's evangelism; that it was through these groups that people were won to the Lord Jesus.

Ouch!

So, there it is. The Bible is all for housegroups and full of them! But here is the rub. Housegroups are not to be simply comfortable and cosy settings for a good natter (or even gossip) among believers (is yours?), but the place where the 'ordinary church member' finds the ministries of the wider church supplemented; the place where Christians are nurtured, discipled and encouraged to reach out to a lost world.

Getting unpacked!

Releasing the Word

Many voices suggest today that preaching is past its 'sell by' date. But nothing could be further from the truth. The people of God have always been indebted to those gifted by God to explain and apply the Scriptures. As evidence we could go back at least as far as Ezra and we can come right up to the present and offer our own personal testimonies of the blessings that we have gained from good Bible teachers. And there is always the supreme example of Jesus himself.

However, Ezra needed the assistance of others who, in smaller groups, helped to explain and apply the word of God. Jesus needed to spend time with his disciples to expound his teaching more fully. In more recent times groups such as the Methodists recognized the importance of 'experience meetings' where (among other things) the Scriptures could be shared in a more intimate setting. At their best, therefore, housegroups ought to provide an environment in which the Scriptures are carefully studied and applied to the needs of its members.

Facilitating prayer

Perhaps you have been to one of those meetings where everyone is encouraged to pray out aloud at the same time. This is one way to encourage all the people of God to pray, especially in large gatherings, but surely not the only way.

This is where 'housegroups' can play such a vital role in the life of the church. Here the first faltering steps in public prayer can be undertaken. Here it is possible to engage in specific intercession in a way that a larger context makes very difficult. Here, perhaps, we can learn that God enjoys us bringing the 'little things' of life to him; and here we can discover that he takes pleasure in answering them too.

Nurturing fellowship

These days I teach at a college where each year I have to get to know sixty or seventy new students. It's a nightmare, little helped by the fact that the psychologists tell me that I have a personality that cannot remember names! Getting to know people is difficult for many of us and the more people around us the more likely it is that we 'go into our shells' and don't get to know anyone at all.

How different it was in the Old Testament extended family. There the group was small enough for everybody to get to know one another, to recognize strengths and weaknesses, to offer assistance and support, to develop skills and to love the 'oddball'; after all, families are like that.

This is surely one of the great values of housegroups; here a fellowship can flourish that enables Jesus' great command to 'love one another' to become a visible reality.

Extending the Kingdom

It was Archbishop William Temple who said that the church is the only organization that exists for the benefit of its non-members. He was, of course, right. The church exists for mission as a fire exists for burning.

Mission should, therefore, be high on the agenda of every congregation; for the great commission was given not to a few specialists but to all the people of God. Yet, especially, in large congregations, mission and evangelism can seem a strange and distant thing which doesn't 'touch base' with the average church member.

It is precisely at this point that the housegroup can be so valuable. There a non-threatening environment can be a stepping-stone for the person interested to find out more about the gospel. There believers can focus upon the needs of specific situations and people (perhaps by 'adopting' a missionary worker). There they can work together in projects that enable them 'in their small corner' to help extend the kingdom. (Have you ever thought of taking your housegroup away to the continent for a weekend's mission?)

Freeing praise

I'm the sort of person who loves to experiment with things; but only in an environment in which I feel secure. I don't think that I am alone. I also believe that where people want to sing about the things of God it is evidence that he is at work in their lives.

So, a housegroup will want to sing together and enjoy 'worship' as a group. And the housegroup is the ideal setting for experimentation and for doing things that are difficult or less effective in a larger setting. Such variety can also overcome the tendency to boredom which some feel if they are singing (again) the same diet that they have had over recent weeks in the main congregation.

This being the case, why not try writing prayers against a meditative musical background, perhaps on the basis of a biblical text? Recently I was involved in a meeting where the orchestrated theme music from *The Lion King* was played over and over again and we were invited to write worshipful lyrics to it. Might your group try something similar?

In fact, there are no lack of ideas and within the context of a housegroup such experiments can sometimes be helpfully made.

Brass tacks

Getting started

So how can a church get housegroups going and functioning effectively? It may seem axiomatic but it is vital that the church leaders, the congregation and the leaders of each group are clear and agreed on what is the purpose of meeting together in housegroups. It seems that far too many churches have set up such groups without asking and resolving such fundamental questions. It is small wonder if aiming at nothing in particular they have unerringly hit the target!

It seems vital that the housegroups have an agreed place within the structure of church life. Thus questions as to whom are the leaders accountable, how are they trained, what are their responsibilities and for what length of time are they to lead a group *etc.* need to have been thoroughly worked through.

Some churches may conclude that (certainly for a period of the church's life) specialist groups may be developed. Might there be a place for a group dedicated to the discipling of young Christians, another dedicated to outreach or mission, another seeking to take maturer believers deeper into the faith?

Most fellowships will probably conclude, however, that groups which gather members of the church from a common geographical area but range in age, experience and so on appear the obvious option. Again, these sort of decisions have to be thought through in advance.

Bible study

Fundamental to the life of the housegroup is the need to meet around the Word of God. Various expedients can be used to choose the most appropriate Scriptures to study. Many congregations have found that digging deeper into and applying the passage which was the focus of the pastor or vicar's sermon the previous Sunday can be helpful. This helps ensure that the message of the text is reflected on and applied to the life of the members of the group. Perhaps certain Scriptures work better if this approach is adopted. After a message on employers and employees based on Ephesians 6:5–9, the congregational members are best able to work out the implications; after all, they say, the minister has probably not done a real day's work for years!

Another method that has worked with success is where the church leader has supplied both a short tape of introduction to be played in each group and some pre-set questions. There are other variations on this: perhaps the group leaders might meet with the church leader responsible and be trained to then go and lead the group. This can be a good pattern (and is a biblical one) since it establishes a framework of training for the whole church. It would not be surprising to discover that this procedure produced a new generation of church leaders!

Where the leadership is hard-pressed to provide such guidance or training (certainly on a regular basis) they might make use of available materials such as the *Crossway Bible Guides*. In such a situation the church would do well to purchase a copy of the study material for each group leader.

The options are endless. What is important is that the Word is studied thoroughly and well and that the study is part of a co-ordinated programme within the church's life.

Prayer

I have sometimes been to prayer meetings where the intercessions have never got beyond praying for gammy knees! Sometimes housegroups too can be very insular in their prayer. But this ought not be so and needn't be so if the group is well led.

Some churches encourage individual groups to 'adopt' a missionary. This is an excellent means of developing a wider prayer interest. But there are other means to develop effective intercession. The sort of ideas offered in chapter 8 of this book should be thought through and acted on. If a housegroup fails to become a focus for concerted intercession it has failed in one of the most important responsibilities placed upon it!

Pastoral care

I recall a situation when a pastor was blamed for his failure to stop a marriage breaking down by the one couple in the church who were actually aware of the problem! The bigger the church, the more likely it is that the leadership will not be able to pick up every emerging pastoral problem; nor should they! The New Testament makes it very clear that the responsibility for pastoral care rests upon every church member (consider what James teaches in 5:19–20). Such can be enormously facilitated by housegroups who are often in a position to be aware of emerging problems before resolution is impossible and where, among friends, appropriate action can be taken.

Not that all pastoral needs are problems. Sometimes pastoral support means no more than doing infirm Mrs Brown's shopping or assisting elderly Mr White with mowing his lawn. However, with the world looking on there is often no better way to demonstrate that 'these Christians love one another'.

If housegroups (especially leaders) need clear guidelines it seems that this is one vital but often neglected area.

Empowered for mission

I remember an occasion in which one member of a housegroup raised questions about what actions the group were going to take as a result of the Bible study they had undertaken. It was as if a bomb had been dropped into the meeting!

Yet if housegroups are to be effective and useful, they ought (must) always be looking to see how they can put discipleship into practice. In many situations, the housegroup is the most natural way in which new congregations can emerge (might this even be the aim in some fellowships?). Even when this is not so, the housegroup is the natural funnel through which others can be added to the church.

So, a housegroup ought to have built into its 'job description' the need to be actively pursuing ways in which its members can individually and together be the means of 'extending the kingdom'.

Thus, within the programme of the group need to be such things as friendship meals, literature distribution *etc*.

In my view, however, the responsibility to evangelize does not begin and end with those around us. To all of us has been given the responsibility to 'reach the world'. In days gone by there were groups such as the 'Women's sewing guilds' which sought to support the work of worldwide evangelization. They proved that 'ordinary people' could have a role to play in the church's task.

These days the housegroup would seem to be an ideal setting within which practical involvement in mission can and ought to be fostered. Some suggestions for achieving this have already been mentioned, but there are others. Many mission organizations now provide regular, detailed prayer resources for their committed supporters. Such bulletins and tapes can be most effectively prayed through within housegroups. But there are also ample opportunities today for short-term mission which include tasks where members can use their practical skills. I think, for example, of a church which sent out a group of available members to redecorate a Christian bookshop on the continent; thus freeing the local workers for work they could best do. France is the most unevangelized country in Europe and it is so nearby. A housegroup might be able to twin with a small congregation in France (they will probably be about the same size) and regularly share and practically support such a work. It is not beyond the capacity of the average housegroup to meet such a challenge.

Indeed, it is my conviction that if groups within the church are not committed to such involvement they are failing to meet one of the fundamental responsibilities that God has placed upon them.

When things go wrong

Many people seem to have a housegroup 'horror story' and these are so prevalent that there is, in certain circles, a reaction setting in against them. This is an understandable but inappropriate reaction since, as we have shown, small groups have a biblical sanction.

Looking inward

Various difficulties do, however, seem to recur. There is the danger of a group becoming inward-looking; a danger into which a whole congregation can sometimes fall. However, we have tried to demonstrate that this is often the result of a failure either in working out what is expected of each group or to give adequate thought to the selection and training of group leaders.

Where the latter occurs and the principles set out above are adopted it is difficult to escape the conclusion that the group will become outward-looking and a place in which God's people are empowered for spiritual growth and active involvement in the work of the gospel.

Mini-churches

Another criticism sometimes made against housegroups is that they can become mini-versions of larger church gatherings and, as a result, an unnecessary luxury. However, we have suggested above that the housegroup is intended to offer something distinctive and supplementary to what takes place elsewhere. Thus, where the aim is to provide the sort of pastoral cover that is not possible in a larger group, where efforts are made to develop individual and corporate prayer and where the housegroup is seen as the cutting edge of the church's evangelism this danger ought to be averted.

Linked with this last criticism is the charge that housegroups can develop a boring sameness about them. It is difficult to escape the conclusion, however, that where this charge is true it reflects a failure of the housegroup to come to terms with the excitement and challenge to radical discipleship which ought to characterize a biblically based and well directed group. As with so many of the charges brought against such groups, critics need to be careful that they do not reject such groups on the basis of their experience of bad examples.

Threat to church unity

Perhaps the most serious charge that is brought against housegroups is that too often they have been a threat to church unity. Individuals, finding themselves big fish in tiny ponds, can exert the power of their personality over the group, sometimes lead it into error and often use it as a springboard for a 'take-over bid' of the church or a basis for dividing from the parent congregation.

These things have occurred far too often for the criticism to be brushed easily aside. So what can be said by way of response? First of all, we need to recognize that this is no new phenomenon. Within the New Testament churches the same sort of thing occurred (1 Timothy, for example, seems to have been written against a background of division between the elders who led the various groups within the church; see 1:3).

Secondly, we have tried to stress throughout this chapter the vital necessity of housegroups being set up properly with a clear understanding of their role and purpose. We can now add to this a further essential requirement in the setting up of the housegroup; the careful choice of leaders. It is usually where a church fails to choose carefully, equip adequately and monitor effectively that problems occur. The choice is not simply to be made on the basis of willingness and the size of the front room!

Thirdly, these group leaders need to be accountable to the overall leadership of the church, whatever form it might take in each church tradition.

But it is easy to focus on the negative. Where groups have succeeded they have often been the way of uniting the church, of deepening its spiritual life and of involving everyone (even those who tend to stand on the edge) in the growth of the fellowship.

As with so many things, we should not reject something that has not always worked before we ask whether failure was inevitable or the result of inadequacies in the preparation for and planning of such groups.

Growing together

This chapter has been written out of a conviction that the church is 'the glorious body of Christ' and, as such, should reflect this in its corporate life. It is assumed that life together will have a corporate focus where the individual believers will meet God as they meet together. It is assumed that central to that corporate life will be the reading, study and explanation of God's self-revelation of himself in the Bible. It is axiomatic that this community will share together around the Lord's Table and will seek to use the gifts that God has given to its members for the building up of the whole body. Scripturally, it seems impossible to escape the fact that true Christian living has the local church as its focus and sees the church as the place of empowering.

It is out of a desire to see all this maximized that housegroups have been 'promoted'. For it is where the members of the church are more closely knit to one another and through this to the wider body, that the church can grow more effectively to maturity and become glorious in reality.

Still sceptical? Do you think that all this is a nice but unreachable ideal? I have sometimes encountered church leaders who are willing to agree that the Bible sets out such a model for church life but reject it by effectively saying, 'It's a nice ideal, but it won't work.' But does God set us unreachable targets or does he not encourage us to look to him for the empowering that alone makes his ideals our realized experience? There is only one possible answer to this question!

Questions

If you are a minister/church leader you might find the following questions helpful if you are considering setting up housegroups:

1. Why do I believe housegroups are necessary?
2. What are the aims and objectives of housegroups and how can they be achieved?

3. How should the housegroups function within the overall life of the church? Who should be the leaders and how are they to be trained? To whom are they accountable?

If you are a group leader (or are about to be asked!) the following questions may be relevant:

1. What is the purpose of the group? How can that purpose best be encouraged?
2. Am I clear what my own job description is? Am I adequately trained for it and am I receiving adequate support? How long am I expected to lead the group? Are there additional resources I need to undertake the work effectively?

If these questions are adequately worked through there is no reason why a housegroup should not be effectively run in your church and be of considerable blessing to it. But careful thought is required to avoid the situation that faced a minister asking a group in another church what their aim was. The answer (after a long pause), 'to keep the meeting going'!

Phil Cuthbert trains and supervises housegroup leaders in Cornerstone Evangelical Church, Nottingham. He also gives consultancy and training to other churches and to businesses. This is an extension of his work with Navigators, where he has served student ministries and churches for over twenty years. Phil lives in a Victorian terraced house with his wife, Lorraine, and their children, Sarah and Andrew. He enjoys (leisurely) sport, logic problems and TV whodunnits and sings in a championship Barbershop Chorus.

The makings of a good housegroup leader

Phil Cuthbert

I once asked a group of church elders what they expected from their housegroups. In no time at all we filled a couple of flipchart sheets with over thirty items ranging from Bible study discussion, through prayer and sharing, worship, social involvement, pastoral care, local evangelism, support of the church's missionaries . . . and anything else they could think of which was not being covered by the Sunday ministry.

I observed that if this was what they expected from housegroups it was also what they expected from their housegroup leaders. Not such a stunning observation, but nevertheless a clear indication as to why this particular church's housegroup leaders were tired, under pressure and in short supply.

Someone has wryly observed that with the resurgence of small groups in the life of the local church we have moved from the need for one omnicompetent minister to the need for many omnicompetent housegroup leaders!

If we are to answer the question at hand, we need first to ask what is a housegroup and what is its main purpose? This issue has been addressed in the previous chapter but I cannot leave it untouched, because we need first to understand something of the purpose of a housegroup before we can say what is expected of its leader.

The purpose of a housegroup

If I were to ask you 'What is a housegroup?' I wonder what you would reply. In my role as a trainer of housegroup leaders the most common concept of a housegroup I encounter is: 'a set of meetings which happen on a (Wednesday) night'. This is shown clearly by the most popular approach to planning for housegroups.

First, the diary comes out. Then the number of programme slots to be filled is calculated. Finally decisions are made as to what will go into the slots to make the meetings interesting and useful.

There is nothing wrong with doing this as such, but it does belong to an institutional view of the church in which the life and work of the church is viewed mainly in terms of the organized activities laid on by the leadership. We should be encouraged to have a more organic view of the church. More of that later.

There is clearly a lot more to a housegroup than a set of meetings. A housegroup is the people and the relationships between the people. Meetings are there to give a context in which to relate to one another biblically. In the meetings we are to encourage and equip one another for life outside the meetings.

We don't meet *at* housegroup any more than we go *to* church. We *are* the church and we *are* the housegroup who meet for specific purposes.

The whole purpose of a housegroup can be seen as being to provide a context for the individual members of the group to grow strong in their walk with God, and together to develop in their ability to relate their faith to everyday life, learning to share their faith with one another and with unbelieving friends, relatives, neighbours and work colleagues.

In short a right expectation on housegroups (and hence on the leaders of housegroups) should be to provide for people's spiritual growth, help them to survive *in* their world, and help them to make an impact *on* their world.

So housegroups are about growth – or at least they should be. Therefore good housegroup leaders will be committed to growth in their own life and in the lives of group members. The times the housegroup comes together (i.e., meetings) will be viewed by the good leader as a specific opportunity for growth.

But how do people grow? How can leaders help others in the group to grow? What can leaders do to provide the right kind of context for healthy growth to take place? Are there particular types of people who will do this better than others?

How people grow

The biblical concept of establishing believers in the faith relates to the ongoing process of bringing a person to maturity in Christ, so that the believer is enabled to stand firm in the faith through all that life doles out.

As members of the Body of Christ we are dependent on him and interdependent on one another if in the end we are to stand. This interdependency between members of the Body is expressed in the mutual help and encouragement we receive from one another. This help should normally occur in three contexts, each with its own distinctive flavour.

The large group is ideal for corporate teaching of biblical truths, inspiring the people of God, motivating them to live for Christ, giving them a sense of being part of the wider body of which Christ is the head, and coming together in corporate worship of him.

The small group is ideal for interacting together over Scripture until we understand it more clearly, for meaningful involvement in each other's lives, for developing our God-given gifts, for sharing our joys and struggles and receiving the 'one-another' ministries of the New Testament.

The one-to-one relationship is ideal for specifically applying the truth of Scripture to an individual's life and situation, for mutual development of character and for a depth of sharing which goes beyond the confines of a group situation.

These three are to work in harmony with each other and feed from each other.

Given this background we can begin to outline some of the qualities which will be displayed by the good housegroup leader.

A facilitator of growth

Good leaders see to it that an atmosphere is created in which people develop relationships of the sort that build up and stimulate one another to faith in God. This is achieved by helping people to develop in their ability to relate to each other openly and honestly about their Christian experience. The format and content of meetings should facilitate this atmosphere, not stifle it. The good leader is aware of the different contexts for growth and thinks of group activities in terms of those aspects best suited to the small-group context.

As well as providing the right context for growth to take place the good leader is able and willing to play their part in the establishing of the individual members of their group. It is not necessary to be perfect in order to do this or be 'better' than others in the group. What *is* necessary is that the leader is willing to be the servant of the group, fulfilling their responsibility as a helper of others.

But what right do we have as leaders to 'interfere' in others' lives. Isn't it safer to stick to organizing a good programme and interesting meetings? It may be safer but it isn't the Bible's view of small-group community. Our basis for meaningful interference in others' lives is firmly rooted in Scripture. A simple study of the 'one-another' statements in the New Testament letters reveals a whole host of ways in which we are encouraged – even commanded to interfere in this way.

Furthermore a closer look at the use of the word 'establish' in the New Testament reveals different agents who are involved in the establishing of a believer: God, the believer and helpers.

Scripture reveals that each has a distinctive role to play: God – e.g., 2 Corinthians 1:21; believer – e.g., James 5:8; helpers – e.g., Acts 18:23 (see diagram).

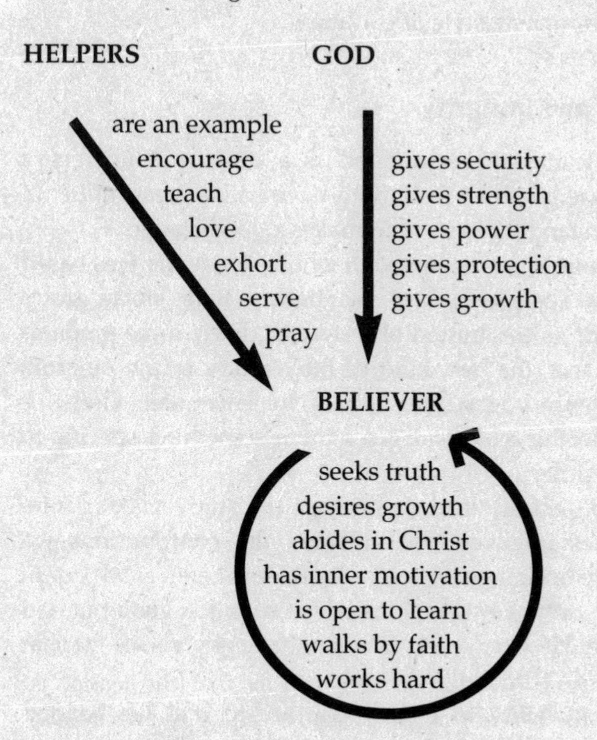

Good leaders have trifocal vision. They fulfil the role of the believer in their own life (looking in), they fulfil the role of helper to their group members (looking out) and they ask God to fulfil his role in their own life and the lives of their group members (looking up). Chiefly they are to be an example to the group as someone who is trying to live a life of ever-increasing devotion to Christ.

John Mallison sums this up by saying that some of the best group leaders he has encountered were marked by certain qualities of character, namely that they were: 'highly motivated to learn and serve and approached all they did with a deep sense of dependency on God.'[1] I like this because it stresses the importance of the character, not the talents of the candidate. The good group leader is one with credibility and integrity, both of which stem from a lifestyle of godliness.

Credibility and integrity

Two group leaders I encountered as a student at university illustrate these qualities well. Both have had a great influence on my understanding as to what makes a good leader.

Ian stood out to me as someone whose whole life was based on the Bible. The group was essentially a Bible study group where each of us committed ourselves to doing some preparation beforehand (the best kind of Bible study in my opinion, because it encourages individuals to encounter God for themselves in the Bible and gives them something specific to bring to the group).

Ian would skilfully lead us through the study making sure everyone was involved. He affirmed the contributions we made, always bringing us back to the Bible whenever we began to ramble on or make statements which sounded good but had no substance. He would ask, 'Do you have any verses for that one'. If we didn't, he did!

Ian had an ability to relate Scripture to real life beyond anything I had previously experienced. This was because whenever he discovered something new in the Bible he did not simply notch it up as something else he knew, but tried to apply it to his life there and then.

In keeping with his passion to see Scripture applied to life Ian once challenged me on an aspect of my behaviour by using a particular verse of Scripture. I challenged Ian as to the true meaning of the verse and we entered into an argument that was resolved only by the use of a Bible dictionary. I won the argument, but he won my respect for his attitude of humility in the face of arrogance (mine), his heart as a learner (compared to my unteachable spirit) and his ever-increasing thirst for and knowledge of the Scriptures (where I relied on my background knowledge and had essentially stopped learning). He had credibility and integrity because he lived what he taught, and he lived by the Bible.

Secondly, there was Richard. If you had asked me if Richard was an appropriate leader of our small group I would have said no. He appeared to me to be lacking in social skills, too young as a Christian (three years compared with the group average of about ten), and far too keen to be admired or copied (these judgments say more about me than Richard!). I did not respect him because he did not fit *my* image of a good leader and did not rate highly on *my* list of admirable attributes.

My struggles came to a head after a study on discipleship. During the discussion Richard said that a true disciple of Jesus would learn from anyone and anything. Those words haunted me that night on my bed. 'Lord, I can't learn from Richard – I don't even respect him. What can I learn from him?'

The next day Richard came bounding into my room and tossed me his little leather wallet in which he kept his memory verses, asking me to check him out on his latest ones. As we talked I became aware of a vital truth. Richard loved me! In fact he loved all of us in the group.

Here was a man so committed to my growth in discipleship that he was spending his life's energies trying to help me do just that. My attitude changed and I learned much from Richard in the two years that followed.

It was Richard who first gave me specific training on how to lead a small-group Bible discussion. He spent hours helping me to devise questions to lead the studies and evaluating their effectiveness afterwards. He encouraged and challenged me, praised and rebuked me, laughed and cried with me, and opened up his life to enable me to see the joys and struggles of what it means to try to live for Christ in this world. He was a living example of Colossians 1:28–29: 'We proclaim him, admonishing and teaching everyone with all wisdom, so that we may present everyone perfect in Christ. To this end I labour, struggling with all his energy, which so powerfully works in me.' We became good friends and I still count it a privilege to have met him before his premature death at the age of twenty-nine from leukaemia.

The testimonies at his funeral served to show that we were not simply part of some leadership training programme he was being put through; this was his way of life . . . love. Richard left a rich legacy in my life which is still paying dividends some twenty years later.

Richard and Ian were good leaders because they had credibility and integrity. Credibility and integrity which came from a developing godly character, a positive servant attitude and genuine spiritual quality which was plain to see. Neither was perfect, their faults were as obvious as their enthusiasm. They were very different people but they had a common attitude and character which were exemplary.

So is it all about attitude and character then? I think mostly yes! As Gareth W. Icenogle comments: 'There is no substitute for spiritual and relational maturity in a small group leader . . . (they) must see their primary empowerment coming from the Spirit, not from their technical knowledge of groups.'[2]

Not everybody, however, with the above qualities makes a good housegroup leader. So what else is involved?

Knowledge about small groups

Small groups are an ideal context for developing relationships with one another, for digging into the Scriptures together, for mutual encouragement in prayer and mutual stimulus in witness.

The style and flavour of each group will be unique, but there are a number of factors which govern the effectiveness and relevance of any group's impact on the life of each member. One of the most important of these is the role of the leaders. Leaders can have a tremendous influence on the inner life of a group and on how any particular group meeting goes.

When considering the qualities of good group leaders it can be helpful to think in terms of development in three important areas – knowledge, attitudes (and character) and skills.

We've already covered much of the ground in terms of attitude, but what about knowledge and skills?

Asking good questions

Most healthy housegroups have at their core some aspect of Bible study. This should not be a mini sermon from one of the group, but a discussion which maximizes the potential of the small group for *interaction* over the Scriptures.

Good leaders help members of the group discover biblical truths for themselves through cultivating the ability to ask the right questions. These questions become the springboard for discussion. There is an art to asking questions; it is not a difficult one to learn, but when learned it will transform a discussion from being stilted – even boring – to a free-flowing interchange of ideas, new discoveries and deep sharing.

Here are three ideas to get you started.

1. Avoid multiple questions, but encourage multiple answers.

How do we get to know God's will, do you sometimes feel he is hiding it from you and what part does counsel from others play?	*becomes*	How do we discover God's will? (Wait – draw out several responses and deal with the other issues later.)

2. Ask open, not closed questions.

Do you think Joseph was angry at his brothers? (Answer – yes or no. The discussion stops until you start it again!)	*becomes*	What feelings do you think Joseph was experiencing? (Lots of answers, use some to develop the discussion.)

3. Use progressive questions to lead the group from discovery, through understanding to application of biblical truth.

Discovery	What does this passage say about love for Christ?
Understanding	How are love and obedience related?
Application	In what specific ways can you demonstrate your love for Christ this week?

Planning and evaluating the questions you ask in the group, will increase your effectiveness as a leader. If you regularly lead discussions, ask another group member to evaluate your use of questions – this will increase their knowledge and awareness as well as developing your skills.

Handling group dynamics

Learning to recognize and use the different sorts of contributions people make is an important part of small-group leadership. When you have a number of different roles being played out in a group, the dynamics can get very interesting. Unless you are aware of the roles people play you will be baffled as to why some discussions go brilliantly and others are awful.

Some people can be very powerful verbally, others very powerful non-verbally. Both can more or less dictate the atmosphere and quality of the group time unless someone recognizes this and responds appropriately. This will be dealt with in more detail in the next chapter, but let me give you an illustration to whet your appetite.

June was in a group I once led. She was totally unaware of the effect she had on the rest of the group. She had a powerful non-verbal influence on the atmosphere. Some people are like that.

Often June would arrive full of enthusiasm and raring to go. Breezing into the room she would sit down with a look which said, 'Right, let's get on with it then, it's going to be a great evening' – and it was! She didn't say anything, but the rest of the group caught her enthusiasm. It was an easy group to lead.

Sometimes June arrived tired, having had a rough day and

not feeling like exerting herself at all. She would flop down in a corner, clearly not in a good mood. Now the look on her face said, 'Do not disturb. I've had a rough day, I do not want to be here, it's going to be a long, tedious evening' – and it was!

June, and the rest of the group were unaware of the effect she had on the dynamics of the group. Once I realized what was happening it was a relatively simple matter to address the issue, either by intercepting June before proceedings began to let her air her frustrations, sympathize and encourage her to look to the Lord for some encouragement through the evening, or to get her involved as quickly as possible to encourage her out of her lethargy.

In both cases it was important to ask God to ensure that his purpose for the evening would not be thwarted, and to help the individual display the right attitude to him and the group.

It is important for leaders to identify and manage the group dynamics in such a way that people are allowed to contribute freely and fully, without hijacking the overall aims of the group which are to do with the learning, growth and development of its members.

When leaders are able and willing to do this, the whole group can be influenced towards a higher and more biblical level of involvement with each other.

If you look at Jesus' dealings with the Twelve in this light, you will observe that he clearly understood the importance of group dynamics and used them to effect a change in the attitudes, beliefs, ideas and behaviour of the disciples (see, for example, Mark 9:33–37 and 10:35–45).

We have seen that housegroups are (or should be) essentially about growth and have explored some of the ways in which people grow. We have observed that the role of leaders is to facilitate growth by the power of their own example and by means of basic small-group knowledge and skills. Now it is time to stand back and take a more panoramic view of the housegroup. For the good leader is one who has an organic, not institutional view of housegroups.

Organic view of the group

The Church is a body with Christ as the head. It is not an organization, though it *has* organization. The same is true of a housegroup. Christ is the true leader of the group, the one head. The leader is not the centre of the group, Christ is. The leader is there to see that the group grows up into Christ and fulfils his will and purpose for them. This is the responsibility of each member of the group. It is the privilege of the leader to serve the group by helping them fulfil their joint and individual responsibilities.

Compare these two lists. Thinking and acting on the basis of the right-hand list rather than the left, will help spread the unrealistic load often felt by housegroup leaders.

Institutional	Organic
Top down ministry	Every member ministry
Adding members	Multiplying disciples
Focused on the church	Focused on the lost
Enslaved to maintenance	Stimulated in mission

Institutional versus organic

Those with an institutional view of the church think in terms of the programme. What jobs need to be done? Who can we get to fill the vacancies? Those with an organic view think in terms of the people. Who has God given? What gifts has he given them? How can these gifts be used for the good of the whole? The end result may be similar in terms of people in jobs, but the process and spiritual impact will be very different.

Top down versus every member ministry

The top down ministry view lays the responsibility for ministry at the door of the professionals. We even call the professionals ministers. The Bible, however paints a different picture. We are all ministers. The so-called professionals are there to equip the rest of us in our ministry, not for us to sit passively under theirs (see Ephesians 4:11–16).

Adding members versus multiplying disciples

The adding members view focuses on getting more people through the door. A full meeting is a good one. Success is measured in terms of numerical growth, not necessarily spiritual quality.

It is striking to observe the way in which Jesus actively reduced the number of his followers. By laying out his terms of discipleship, and by refusing to water down the truth about himself he sifted out the true followers from the half-hearted. Have a look at John 6:25–69 if you find that difficult to believe. Jesus' strategy was to focus on multiplying faithful disciples who would in turn reach others.

Focus on the church versus focus on the lost

To be focused on the church is right and good, but if our focus is *only* inward we miss the whole point of our being the church in the world. Jesus' main focus was on the lost, so should be ours. It would be a good thing to evaluate all our church and housegroup activities in terms of their effectiveness in enabling us to reach the lost.

This has implications on all sorts of areas. One felt keenly by many housegroup leaders is that of pastoral care. They feel responsible for the problems and needs of their group members. In the New Testament pastoral care is viewed in terms of a busy hospital rather than a comfortable hospice. The aim of pastoral care is to keep the troops in good shape for the battle, not give full time intensive care for the terminally ill.

As Stephen Gaukroger puts it: 'Paul sees the role of overseer as a protector against false teaching. Even the pastoral image of shepherd is used in the context of protection against wolves. Many Christians today see leaders as being available to meet their needs and solve their problems. Paul sees them protecting from attack, so the ministry of evangelism can continue. Shepherds are to feed, lead and protect the sheep . . . not to carry them!'[3]

When the focus is outside the group, on the lost to be reached, the group is more likely to fulfil its God-given purpose.

Maintenance versus mission

It is not altogether fair to set these two against each other. Both have their place. But think of it as an extension of the previous point. If we become enslaved to maintenance our gaze will necessarily be forced inwards. If we discipline ourselves to look out in response to God's call to reach our generation for Christ, many things we thought necessary to maintain become superfluous to requirements and the chains of slavery are broken!

Leaders who learn to view their group in this way will focus on developing the gifts of group members, seeing them put to work within the group and beyond; they will think in terms of growth in quality and they will experience growth in numbers; they will develop others in leadership in preparation for the time when 'one group will become two'; and their own personal efforts to live and speak for Christ will be mirrored in the attitudes and actions of their group members, for it remains true that we multiply after our own kind.

Notes

1 John Mallison, *Growing Christians in Small Groups* (Scripture Union, 1989), p. 37.
2 Gareth Weldon Icenogle, *Biblical Foundations for Small Group Ministry* (Inter Varsity Press, 1989), p. 215.
3 Stephen Gaukroger, *Acts: Free to Live* (Crossway Books, 1993), p. 173.

John Earwicker is Church Life Director for the Evangelical Alliance, and a member of EA's strategic leadership team. He has taught and written about housegroups, has worked with Youth for Christ and lectured at the University of Birmingham. He is married to Heather. Their children are Simon, a school teacher and Jessica, a theology student. John and his wife are doing an evening class together, learning badminton. They also enjoy travelling, photography and admiring art and architecture.

The skills of leadership

John Earwicker

Let's face it. Most people feel that they could lead a small group. Some of your own housegroup members may even think that they could do a better job than you! The issue that concerns us in this chapter is not 'can I lead a housegroup?', but 'can I lead a housegroup well?'

On the underground in London recently, a poem appeared that reflects this desire to lead and the question of the necessary skills.

> I would like to be a leader.
> I want to be a leader.
> Can I be a leader?
> Can I? Can I?
> Promise? Promise?
> Yipee! I'm the leader!
> OK. What shall we do?
>
> (Roger McGough, in *Poems on the Underground* (Cassell, 1996))

Desire for leadership is all too evident in these lines. But this aspirant's first act of leadership is to ask his group what they want to do! Is this skill or folly?

Measuring skill levels is tough in any area. For football, how many points you collect over a season would be a guide. In bargain hunting, you might be able to add up how much is saved during a year. Leading a group is rather trickier. Perhaps one way to think about it would be to reflect on how effective the group is in achieving its purposes.

In the film *Kes*, an ageing schoolmaster is shown taking a football lesson with his young pupils. He runs out on to the field ahead of them. Not only is he the referee, but he plays as captain of a team as well. This is not unlike the housegroup leader who is both a participant and the person with the authority to 'blow the whistle'. Our fictional schoolmaster abuses his power as the referee to enable himself as a player to score a penalty that wins his team the imaginary Wembley final. As leader, he is using the pupils to work out his own fantasy. The pupils learn very little about football but the leader is happy! The very opposite of the Bible's vision of servant leadership.

The ultimate joy of the servant leader of a small group is to know that the group recognizes that it is achieving its agreed aims.

In this chapter we review four basic needs for the housegroup leader to understand:

- the purpose of the housegroup
- the way that small groups work
- how adults learn
- the nature of the skills needed by an effective housegroup leader.

Understanding the housegroup's purpose

Most churches have housegroups. Fewer are exactly sure as to *why* they have them. During the early 1980s, Eddie Gibbs taught extensively on church growth. His most famous commentary on housegroups was that 80% of all growing churches had housegroups. Once his audience had duly noted this fact, he would then inform them that 80% of all declining churches had housegroups too!

Be clear about purpose

It's not having a housegroup that makes the difference. Clarity of purpose for such a small group is what counts. Sadly, many churches run housegroups for a confusing multiplicity of reasons. When a rationale for having housegroups has been intentionally worked through, all too frequently it involves so many aims as to be unhelpful, unclear and unattainable. Clarity of purpose is vital in choosing among so many possible activities that the group could undertake. It is vital in determining how frequently and for how long the group should meet.

Often, housegroup leaders are only informed of the purpose or plethora of purposes for the housegroup they are being asked to lead. A good leader will seek to be involved in *negotiating the declared priority purpose* of the small group which she or he is being asked to lead.

In talking with senior church leaders, the leader will need to clarify:

- the priority purpose as perceived by those persons
- the expectations they have of the housegroup leader for achieving this purpose
- how it is proposed to determine effectiveness of achievement, and
- how the housegroup structures relate to the church's other adult discipleship programmes.

If senior church leadership is unable or unwilling to be clear about the priority of the housegroup, the leader will have to continue the dialogue. Besides explaining the difficulty of being unclear about priorities and the danger that this poses for effective action, external advice might be asked for.

Build ownership of purpose

'Building ownership' is vital to the group's performance. Even in the most authoritarian kind of church, genuine and lasting effectiveness is only possible where aims are genuinely owned by members.

The truly skilful housegroup leader will be concerned to allow members of the group to explain their views about the purpose as worked through by the senior leadership. Rather than brainstorming lots of additional purposes, the housegroup leader will invite the group to consider the reasons for the particular purpose statement and explore its meaning.

She or he will ask questions about the way the group feels towards this purpose and to explore any conflicts of interest that may be identified. The skilful leader will not impose or insist on matters at the outset and will honestly seek to be the go-between. This involves neither criticizing the senior church leadership's vision nor ignoring valid contributions from his small-group members. *The skilful housegroup leader is a mediator.*

Review activities against purpose

All groups can get stuck into a rut. Habit is important in the life of any group, but not all habits are good ones.

I know of a housegroup which had 'fellowship' as its nebulous purpose statement. What the senior leadership meant by this was practising Bible study and prayer. What the housegroup host understood by the same term was increasingly elaborate snacks. The snacks grew ever closer to being meals that left little time for the study! The group got bigger in every way but didn't make a lot of progress in wisdom and discernment!

The role of the housegroup leader is to take stock on a fairly regular basis (certainly every term). There will be reflection on the type and balance of activities and their effectiveness in helping the group fulfil its purpose.

A good leader will obtain the views of the group about this, either formally or informally. Formal review can be conducted verbally with the whole group or by questionnaire. Informal means usually involve discussions on a one-to-one basis or with sub-sets of the group. Questions from the leader can explore the feelings and opinions of group members. The leader will share the findings of the review with the members and encourage them to make the necessary adjustments to the activities of the group. In some instances, this may lead to a renegotiation with senior church leadership on the priority purpose for the housegroup.

Understanding how small groups work

When small groups meet, more goes on than meets the untrained eye. We know this from experience in our human families as well as within church circles.

For example, youth groups are not only about learning more about the Christian faith. They are also places where boys get to meet girls, teenagers escape from parents and youth leaders express their frustrations with those who once led them!

So what does go on in small groups? The average housegroup leader tries to be attentive to the *content* of the group meeting. A lot of time goes into preparing a Bible passage, group discussion questions or prayer topics. By content, we mean the formal, known subject to be addressed. The content is what most people will focus on consciously. On the surface of things, it can appear to be the priority. But whenever groups of any size meet, there are also *processes* at work. Already, the sensitive group leader knows that how you lay out the chairs and whether you have refreshments has some influence on how things work out. These are important issues, which we will reflect on later. But there are even more important factors at work.

Small groups are made up of people. And people are different! When you put them together, things happen beyond what they are asked to do. Effective housegroup leaders are people who 'read' groups; who think not only about the content of what is being done but also about the processes that can be observed and influence performance.

In a housegroup setting, some of the factors that influence behaviour include:

- temperament and preferred roles
- motivation and commitment
- life circumstances.

We will take a brief look at each of these aspects, though further reading and other forms of training will be necessary to develop lasting skills in these areas.

Character

People have roles (appropriate, related patterns of behaviour) which they prefer to adopt because of their temperament or type of personality. For all of us, there are circumstances where we feel different levels of comfort or competence. If you take very competent infants' teachers and ask them to work with disaffected teenagers, they will struggle. Ask big-platform speakers to address ten people in a home-based coffee morning and they will be uncomfortable. Put a brain surgeon and a refuse collector in the same group and they will need time to understand each other's concerns. In any group, people will assume one or more roles, some more consciously than others. Some are naturally concerned to see the other person's point of view. Others enjoy a good row for the fun for it! Knowing your group and understanding what makes them behave as they do is a key to effective leadership.

The Billy Graham team teach about enquiry groups after major missions. They identify unhelpful roles that people can play in groups. These include:

Chattering Charlie who talks so much that no-one else can contribute;
Silent Sam who is quite the reverse;
Humble Henry who won't answer because he isn't sure but hates being wrong;
Prickly Pete who gets worked up but cannot recognize his anger;
Red herring Robert who constantly side-tracks discussion; and
Jimmy Joker who often jokes to hide his own embarrassment or relieve his own tension.

A skilful leader will learn to identify temperament and preferred roles in people. In particular, such a leader will reflect on where such temperaments and roles may clash and develop plans for dealing with such situations.

Commitment

Thought and prayer will also need to be given to the variation which will exist among group members in their motivation and level of commitment. One of the most significant differences that can exist in any group is between what the small-group experts refer to as *task and social orientation*. At its simplest, this means that some people are committed to the group for the sake of the task whereas others are committed to the group for its own sake, irrespective of the purpose, concentrating on interpersonal enjoyment. Obviously, many people exhibit varying combinations of these preferences.

Knowing your group in these terms will be very helpful. It is not necessary to change these orientations in people, but very necessary to understand them. When the group is struggling to be united over any issue, the social orientation members will be of greatest help to the leader. This is reversed when achieving a specific aim is under threat.

Evidently, in any housegroup, there will also be different levels of Christian commitment which will influence the way the group behaves.

Circumstances

The life circumstances of group members also influence their interaction. The threefold personal aspects of body, mind and spirit have a great influence on the working of the group. Often, church housegroups are acutely aware at the level of spirit but oblivious to the other two facets of each member. The body plays a significant role in the dynamics of any group. Tiredness, injury, illness or disability are factors which influence the way people relate. These physical elements are overlooked in a group at the risk of producing an ethereal, irrelevant spirituality.

Mind is also significant. Some people live their lives primarily in this part of their anatomy! For others, it is seldom engaged! And between such extremes are the majority. What a person knows and the way they have been taught to think are key elements in group life.

There are those who advocate groups made up of people who share similar interests and backgrounds. There is strong evidence that such groups produce greater growth, at least numerically, but many of our 'brainiest' members may need considerable help from others in understanding their emotions, for instance. The wise housegroup leader is sensitive to interpersonal differences and knows how to draw out the varied mental, physical and emotional giftings in the group as appropriate to the general purpose and specific tasks of the moment.

Groups change too!

Groups are just like people; they change over time. It is the leader who has the responsibility to help the group to gel and grow. Others may assist (or obstruct!) this development; but the leader must assume responsibility.

One of the most helpful secular approaches to understanding groups in this regard is by Bruce Tuckman[1]. Having reviewed a great deal of research in this area, he demonstrates that, in most cases, *small groups move through four phases of development*. He identifies these phases as: forming, storming, norming and performing.

The desired goal of the development process is *performing*. In this phase, the group has resolved its social inter-relationship difficulties and is pulling together harmoniously in fulfilling the purpose for which it is intended. The roles of group members are exercised in a complimentary manner. The group is effective. Not every group reaches this fourth and most fulfilling stage. Those that do are likely to have taken some considerable time working through the previous three stages.

The third stage which Tuckman identifies is that of *norming*.

By norming, he refers to the group beginning to 'gel'. The group feels a unity, a cohesiveness. Group members have adjusted their roles to one another and group 'rules' (known as norms) are clearly understood.

The stage prior to this is called *storming*. In this phase, there can be open or covert conflict around interpersonal issues. Group pressure or the requirements of the task are resisted. Emotions can run high or are close to the surface.

The initial phase he labels as *forming*. Here, members of the group can exhibit a great deal of dependence on the leader and even on others in the group whom they already know. People will 'test' each other as they try to orientate themselves to one another and the task.

Not all groups proceed through these stages at the same rate. Groups regress as well as progress. Certainly the shared values of a group of Christians can make some of the storming/norming aspects a little smoother than might otherwise be the case. Nevertheless, similar behaviours can be observed in many housegroups.

As the group begins to form, the leader must resist being over-depended upon, especially by one sub-group over another. The leader will explain and affirm supportive, clarifying, exploratory behaviours.

In the storming phase, the leader will need to defend the weakest, oppose the insensitive and hold the ring. The task is to help the group understand its need of shared expectations. There may be a strong pastoral need to pick up those who are offended or surprised at the group's behaviour.

In the norming phase, the leader reflects back to the group and supports the progress that has been made. By the performing phase, the leader will be much more in the background, enjoying the fruit of all the agony that has gone before!

So, *the skilful housegroup leader seeks to understand what stage of development the group has reached, needs to interpret behaviour accordingly and attempts to enable growth to higher levels of functioning.*

Understanding how adults learn

Just when you thought being a skilful housegroup leader could not possibly get any more difficult, a new issue emerges. The fact is that adults learn in different ways from one another, and you can't ignore these learning factors.

Generalizations

John Daines[2], a senior lecturer in adult education at the University of Nottingham, has identified a number of generalizations about adults as learners. Some of them are very significant for church housegroups.

Adult learning is more likely to occur when the material is relevant to the individual and/or where it can be linked to what is already known. However, adults require time – and sometimes help – to recognize relationships between the new and the already known and to make the appropriate connections.

Adults can be expected to assume responsibility for themselves. They join a group freely and they may not respond too well to being told what to do without good reason.

They are likely to lack confidence in themselves as learners and to underestimate their own abilities. They tend to be over-anxious and reluctant to risk making mistakes. Above all they will not want to fail or look foolish. They need to identify and work to realistic goals that are within their capabilities and then experience some ongoing success in attaining them.

Adult learners respond to tutors who show genuine interest and concern in individual achievements, who support and encourage them, and who interact with them on equal terms.

Adults learn best when:

- they feel secure and they can try things out in safety
- their needs are being met in ways that they can see are relevant and appropriate
- they know what they have to do
- they are actively involved and engaged
- they know how well they are doing

- they see and experience that they are welcomed and respected both as adults and as individuals in their own right.

The skilful housegroup leader provides an environment that fosters adult learning.

Particularities

Some people enjoy small-group debate. Others (including some of your small-group members) do not enjoy this approach. They may prefer to read something or learn by getting their hands dirty. In her helpful book, *Learning for Life*, Yvonne Craig[3] reviews the work of two Americans, Kolb and Frey, and of two Britons, Honey and Mumford. Their work suggests a cycle of learning among adults in which we all have a preferred style or styles.

Experience is one example of how we learn. All that we do has a potential for learning. It may depend on our recognizing the relevance or connectedness of the moment. *Activists* focus on experience. They learn through challenges and variety.

Reflection is another part of the learning cycle. This involves pondering our experience and making sense of its variety. *Reflecters* need time and space to think, to prepare, to research. They prefer not to take risks, even while taking a broad view.

The cycle includes *reviewing* and fitting things into a coherent framework. Such adults are *theorists* who prefer logic to emotion; complexity to simplicity. They like things to be neatly tidied up into a system.

Action is an integral part of the learning cycle. *Pragmatists* learn by practice, preferring to deal with things closely related to their most pressing circumstances. They pick up ideas quickly when relevant but get impatient with long-winded discussion or complex theory.

All of these styles are likely to be present in your group. What is sure is that you will not please all of them all of the time. As leader, you must try not to impose your own preferred learning style on the entire group.

The effective leader considers how each adult in the housegroup learns and ensures a variety of approaches to learning so as to encourage each member.

Understanding the skills you need

By now, you are conscious of some of the complexities of being a skilful housegroup leader. These should not be allowed to overwhelm you, however. Not only does the Holy Spirit promise to teach us, but we are surrounded by people who are making small groups function well. Dependence on God and talking with more experienced small-group leaders are available to all of us.

The skills which we need to lead any small group include: listening, observing and facilitating. The skills particular to a church housegroup such as study and outreach are dealt with in other chapters.

Listening

Listening in a group requires attention to what is being said, what isn't being said, who is speaking and who isn't.

The leader of a small group should listen attentively. Not only is this a matter of courtesy but also a matter of learning. It is very discouraging to any speaker if it appears that she or he is not being listened to. When listening is especially important in a group, the leader can underline this by asking someone to take notes or by using a tape recorder (though this might have the effect of silencing the speaker! Be sensitive.). The effective leader learns not only to listen to the words but also to the tone of voice. 'Come here', can be said softly and seductively or loudly and angrily. The tone of voice conveys both meaning and motivation.

The skilful leader is also 'listening' to what is not being said. People vary enormously in their verbal openness. Some people within minutes of meeting a stranger will confide their life history and its intimate details, whereas others can take years to share sensitive thoughts and emotions. The caring leader will get to know the various group members in this way and develop appropriate ways to curb some and draw out others, depending on the needs of the moment.

In any group, verbal assertiveness varies.

In this respect, it is important to remember that the larger the group, the more likely it is to be dominated (verbally especially) by a smaller proportion of the people. In other words, in a group of three, all are likely to speak. In a group of twenty, perhaps only four will make significant contributions.

Observing

Observing in a group is all of a piece with listening. It involves being alert to what is being done, what is not being done and by whom. In the matter of observation, the astute leader will pay attention to body language and eye contact.

Body language simply refers to how people position themselves. This refers both to personal posture (for example, head held either close to the chest with eyes down or very erect but with glazed eyes) and position in relation to the group (for example, leaning forward with eye intensity showing engagement or sitting apart and backwards in the seat, eyes averted showing non-involvement).

The leader needs to be aware of body language to learn about group members and decide how to intervene or influence what is happening. So leaders who see most of the group asleep might consider trimming their monologue!

Eye contact is an especially important aspect of body language. Although people vary in the extent to which they seek and give eye contact, such interactions can suggest the extent to which people are open to one another. In general, a group that is well established and performing effectively will have frequent and sustained interpersonal eye contact which is relatively evenly spread among all the members. By contrast, a new group will tend to have brief eye contacts focused especially on the formal leader.

Facilitating

Facilitating a group in achieving its purpose requires the skills of listening and observing. It goes beyond them, however, because it is concerned with interacting with the group to help it fulfil its purposes. It represents the effective deployment of your listening and observing skills mixed with wisdom.

It is clear that you cannot alter people's behaviour in a short space of time. However, you do have primary responsibility (or should have) for three key elements:

- the programme
- the environment
- your own behaviour.

The leader should involve the group in considering the nature of the programme to be followed. He or she will also give consideration to the needs, life circumstances and gifting of the group. In particular, the group leader should assume responsibility for questions of learning styles and level of participation and leadership by other group members.

The environment is important. The size of room, type and distribution of chairs, level of heat and light all influence performance. An intimate setting is more helpful in sharing emotions whereas a less intimate setting is preferable for the transfer of information. The group leader must assume responsibility for this and not leave such matters to chance.

In relation to self, the skilful group leader will reflect on these questions:

- what are my own strengths and weaknesses in helping the group achieve its purpose?
- how am I perceived by group members?
- do I know where the group is in its life development and am I leading appropriately for that phase?
- do I understand why the group members behave as they do?
- am I affirming the behaviours that help the group and intervening to overcome negative behaviours?

- am I ensuring a variety of learning opportunities or do we do the same kind of activity all the time?

While it is true that some people have a natural capacity to think in these terms, it is possible to learn and develop such skills. There are ways of handling shy or domineering people in the group. It is possible to become more sensitive to group processes and to ask people to provide you with their observations of your performance.

Perhaps the most vital need in any housegroup leader is that their personal relationship with God is such that they know themselves and know that they are accepted by him. They do not need to use the group to attain a sense of fulfilment but can serve it and rejoice in its success.

Delight in the growth of others is at the heart of skilful small-group leadership.

Notes

1 Bruce Tuckman, 'Developmental Sequence in Small Groups', in *Group Processes* ed. Peter B. Smith (Penguin, 1970).

2 John Daines, Carolyn Daines and Brian Graham, *Adult Learning Adult Teaching,* Department of Adult Education (University of Nottingham, 1988).

3 Yvonne Craig, *Learning for Life* (Mowbray, 1994).

4

Steve Motyer currently teaches at London Bible College, and pastors a church in Watford in his 'spare' time! He has had experience of house groups of various sorts during twenty years' ministry in different churches. He has a wife and three teenage children, and enjoys cycling and playing the piano. He is one of the editors of the* **Crossway Bible Guides** *and is very enthusiastic about their potential in spreading Bible knowledge and supporting the exciting ministry of house-groups worldwide.

Teaching the Bible in small groups

Steve Motyer

I remember vividly the church Bible study I attended in my teens. My Dad was the vicar, and our living-room was stuffed with chairs, all in rows, angled towards the fireplace where Dad sat at a little table. The pattern was always the same. Opening hymn, then Bibles open and straight into the study. My father is a brilliant Bible expositor (that's the old word for it), so for half an hour or so he would talk and we would listen, usually spell-bound. I particularly remember going through Amos, passage by passage, week after week. He later used the same material to give the Bible readings at the Keswick convention, and then turned it into the IVP *Bible Speaks Today* volume on Amos.

Then after the exposition, we would pray: needs would be shared, and prayer would flow in response to the message he had drawn out of the passage.

It was great! I was fed by those sessions, and so were we all. I remember the deep thankfulness in Daisy Shepherd's prayers. She was a lovely old lady, well into her eighties, who had come to faith late in life through my Dad's ministry. How she praised God for the Good News which had come to mean so much to her. She never missed the church Bible study.

Yes, it was great. *But why doesn't that formula work any more*? I think it was unusual even then, in the sixties. In the nineties, it is just not where it's 'at', in group Bible study – which is a shame for those of us to whom talking comes naturally! Why has the expository Bible study fallen out of fashion, and is this decline a good thing? At first sight, it matches a teaching aim perfectly: if the purpose of the Bible study is to teach the Bible, then surely the best formula will be to find a good Bible teacher and simply launch him or her in front of the group . . . Yes?

No. I can think of three reasons why this formula has faded, and all of them point towards the need for something different.

- You have to have an unusual teaching gift, to be able to sustain people's attention for half an hour or more at the end of a tiring day. In fact you have to be really brilliant, to make just listening to you the best way for people to spend half an hour's Bible study.
- Groups have multiplied in local churches and they can't all have the vicar to lead them. Many leaders simply could not give an extended exposition and yet they still need to be able to teach the Bible in a group setting. How can it be done? That's what this chapter is all about!
- People are now much less willing just to sit and listen. In every other area of life – politics, education, business, the civil service – old patterns of authority have broken down and people have come to expect a much more co-operative, consultative, even accountable style of leadership. This has spin-offs in church life! And as far as group Bible study is concerned, this is a good thing: for in the long run people remember what they discover for themselves, or thrash out in discussion, far better than what they simply hear from someone else, however good a teacher.

But this makes life difficult for group leaders. On the one hand, you need to be able to communicate the exciting content of the Bible to your group. But on the other hand, you need to do this in a way that suits their learning styles and the 'ethos' of the group – which in all likelihood is also a caring and fellowship group. If the people in your group are keen to share their needs and express their care for each other, then that very 'ethos' will make teaching difficult. We've all been there: the Bible study which goes round and round in circles as everyone chips in with the first thoughts that come into their heads. Self-expression is fine, up to a point. But in the end people feel dissatisfied if they go away feeling that they have spent an hour sharing each other's ignorance, as well as each other's needs for prayer.

What's the answer? We need *methods of teaching* which are not just adapted to a 'group sharing' setting and ethos, but actually build upon it as an advantage to be exploited, and not a disadvantage to be outweighed! In other words, you are not going to be a successful teacher in a group session if you simply tack a bit of discussion on to a talk by you. This will affect how you prepare for the Bible study. Sorry! If you go into the Bible study with the same kind of notes that you would use to give a talk, failure looms (I speak from experience!). This chapter aims to give some tips about avoiding that failure. There are five vital factors to bear in mind and work at: the vital *principle, strategy, preparation, methods* and *skills.*

The vital principle – *interactive learning*

This is what the hard-pressed group leader must aim for, all the time: to enable people actually to learn *through* their engagement with each other in the group, and not to have their learning hindered by the presence of others. A hard principle to translate into practice, but one which actually matches Paul's teaching about the church as 'the Body of Christ'.

Paul puts it in a nutshell in Colossians 3:16: 'Let the word of Christ dwell in you richly as you teach and encourage one another with all wisdom, and as you sing psalms, hymns and spiritual songs with gratitude in your hearts to God.' This is remarkable in three ways:

1. This former Pharisee, who is now an apostle, does not tell the Colossians to listen only to him or to the 'authorized' teachers in their church, but *to each other also.* He trusts the presence of the Holy Spirit in the church to give 'wisdom' to all. He was only too aware that such 'wisdom' does not come automatically. It

has to be *acquired*, as the church in Corinth painfully discovered. The Colossian Christians need to be inhabited by 'the word of Christ', to shape their minds and hearts. But Paul does not put them on probation until they show signs of having 'the word of Christ' within them. He encourages mutual teaching *now.*

2. See how Paul connects teaching with *encouragement*. 'Heads only' Bible studies are not for him. He wants teaching which will make stronger disciples, and not just cleverer Christians.

3. And see how he connects teaching and encouragement with *worship*, specifically, the heart-felt, thankful singing of songs which express the truths with which they must encourage each other. In fact, so closely does Paul connect all these things that we could put it like this: *it is supremely in shared worship that a group of Christians can teach and encourage each other*. This thought is expressed even more clearly in Ephesians 5:19, where Paul tells us that we *speak to each other* when we sing, communicating the truths that bind us to each other and to Christ.

This is not to say that 'head-based' discussion and study are wrong – far from it. But Paul would clearly be uneasy about a housegroup, or church, or theological college, where the teaching and learning did not have a *worship focus*. For more details see the next chapter by Chris Bowater.

So for Paul *interactive learning* means mutual participation in sharing, and worshipping around, the great truths of the faith.

The vital strategy – *clearly defined goals*

Let me put you on the spot. The last time you led a Bible study, did you decide beforehand exactly what you wanted to achieve with your group through the meeting?

You don't have to tell the group what your aims are. Sometimes this may be helpful, in order to concentrate their minds on a distinct goal. But often it may be better to keep your aims private, because you may not achieve them! – and it will be demoralizing for the group to feel that they have let you down. But you yourself must decide beforehand the destination to which you want to lead the group, during the coming session. Unless you decide this clearly it will be hard to avoid a circular ramble.

Your goal can be *educational*, *devotional*, or *practical*.

An educational goal involves ideas. You decide that, above all else, you want to communicate certain ideas or truths. For instance, in preparing a session on Philippians 2:1–11, you have become so excited by the sheer grandeur of its picture of Jesus Christ, that your aim becomes simply to help people to grasp it for themselves, as you have done.

A devotional goal involves responses towards God. This does not leave the mind aside, of course. But you might decide that, beyond *understanding* the passage, your group needs to move on to make definite *responses* to it. You might be studying Paul's teaching about prayer in Philippians 4:1–9, for instance, and you decide that it will be vital for your group to base a prayer-time on the passage. Or you are studying 1 John 1, and decide that you want the group to leave thoroughly forgiven! So you focus the session on a time when they all write down their sins and then prayerfully burn them on a communal fire.

A practical goal involves activities. The activity can be just discussion – for instance, in response to Ephesians 5:3–14 you might get them to discuss what advice the church should give to its young people about their regular trips to the cinema. Or in response to Matthew 19:3–12 they might discuss what the church could do locally to support and protect marriages. Or you could decide that they should actually *do* something – write and perform a sketch, plan an act of worship, write letters to church missionaries, fund-raise – the possibilities are endless. The chapters on 'creative ideas' in this book give lots of suggestions.

Some aims will be suggested naturally by the passage you are studying. And whatever aim you have it must flow out of the passage, so that people are aware that they are responding to the Scriptures, and not just to your leadership. But you will need to decide what aim to have in the light of the needs of your group and where you know they are 'at', spiritually and personally.

These goals are not mutually exclusive. You will always want the group to seek out the meaning of the passage, so there will always be an *educational* element. And if you are seeking to follow the basic principle outlined above, then there will always be a *devotional* element: you will always set the study in the context of worship. The point I am making here concerns the *focus* of your aim for the session, the goal which everything else will serve.

The vital hour – *productive preparation*

Housegroup leaders are usually busy people, faced with the challenge of carving out time for preparation in an already crowded life. One of our chief aims in producing the *Crossway Bible Guides* has been to help group leaders to make their limited preparation time *truly productive*. Here are the crucial points to bear in mind:

1. You cannot lead a Bible study on *no* preparation, even with a *Crossway Bible Guide* in your hand. Sorry! It just can't be done.
2. Hopefully the most vital element in the preparation will already have been done well in advance, possibly by or with the help of others: each individual study will be part of a wider *programme of study* which the group is following. Many churches set up a common programme for all their groups, and this is highly commendable. In such cases you will know already what the overall aim for the programme is, and how each session fits into it. But if you are in charge of the overall programme for your group, remember that this really is the most vital preparatory stage, to which much care and prayer needs to be given. You need to do it with the advice and support of others, if possible.

If, for instance, you are planning a term's sessions, then you need to do three things:

- decide what to study;
- discover what resources are available either for the whole group to have, or just for yourself; and

- plan the programme, specifying a preliminary aim for each session.

This will take some time! It may have been done for you by the leadership of your church. If you have to do it yourself, encourage yourself with the thought that time *invested* in planning the programme carefully will eventually be time *saved* when it comes to preparing each session.

We have tried to make the *Crossway Bible Guides* as helpful as possible here. Generally speaking, we have divided the books of the Bible into programme-length sections which are in turn sub-divided into individual studies with questions attached. This means that, if you want to, you can plan the programme for your group around the longer sections, and then use the individual studies and questions flexibly in the light of your group and its needs.

3. See 'The vital strategy' above: the crucial step in your preparation for each meeting will be *deciding the aim* for the session.

4. Even if you are in charge of the coming session, you can still use others within it. Why not give small assignments to others in the group, ahead of the meeting? This is a good way of training future leaders. With enough notice, most people are capable of researching some specific points for the group; for instance, what was it like to be a prisoner in New Testament times? or a slave? If your whole group has acquired *Crossway Bible Guides* for themselves, or some other study guide, you can set tasks for them all ahead of the meeting.

5. Make yourself thoroughly familiar with the passage. If you have done the things above, you will already know it to some extent. Now soak yourself in it, and keep asking questions about it. Here's the secret you need to know: the question 'Why?' is the most vital in Bible study. I sometimes wonder whether God gets as exasperated with me as I used to, when my small children kept responding to my explanations with yet another 'Why?' I hope he doesn't, because that question really is the key to discovery. Ask 'why?' about everything in the passage.

For instance, if you are studying Matthew 11:28–30, these are the 'whys' you might ask: Why does Jesus make this appeal at this point in his ministry? Why does he address 'you who labour and are heavy-laden'? Why does he use the picture of a 'yoke'? Why does he echo the words of Jeremiah 6:16 in his appeal? Why does he say his yoke is easy, when it is often so difficult to follow him? Why does he mention his own character in the middle of verse 29, 'I am gentle and humble in heart'?

6. Such questions will send you scurrying off to find help. There are many aids available – not just *Crossway Bible Guides*! If your time is limited then you may not be able to do very much research. But if you do it with your questions firmly in mind, then you can make sure that your research is directed towards what you want to know – even if the books you consult don't answer them! You may be left with unanswered questions, but don't worry. You don't need to know everything in order to lead a good Bible study. Some excellent resources to mention are the *NIV Study Bible* (Hodder & Stoughton), and the *New Bible Commentary 21st Century Edition* (IVP): this is a one-volume commentary on the whole Bible, so the material on each passage is necessarily brief but designed to get right to the heart of things. A good 'background' resource is useful to have, too: the IVP *New Bible Dictionary* or the Lion *Handbook to the Bible* can provide essential background information quickly.

7. Now plan the session, matching the passage to your goal. You may want to modify your goal in the light of what you have discovered, especially if God has spoken to you or laid some specific need or vision on your heart. How will you actually spend that hour? This is where you might want to start writing things down to help yourself to lead the meeting. It is good to plan it through the eyes of the group: what will *they* spend the hour doing, and how will *they* move through that hour to the destination you have in mind for them?

Plan the hour in notional blocks of time, and give a time-allocation to specific teaching goals. Your plans may go out of the window, but that's the nature of groups!

8. In deciding these things, you will draw on your teaching skills, and the next two points are designed to give some help here – although we hope that this whole book will equip you with the skills you need to lead successfully. In particular chapter 7 by Dave Cave provides much creative guidance about how to communicate the Bible imaginatively to groups.
9. Finally, the most important point of all. The whole process of preparation needs to be bathed in *prayer*. For *yourself*: you will teach most effectively the things which God has taught you, personally, through the passage. For the *session*: you need to be listening carefully to him for direction as you plan it. And for the *group:* as you pray for them, your love for them will be strengthened, and that is the vital foundation of the whole exercise.

The vital methods – *group teaching resources*

By 'resources' I do not just mean practical aids, but also the sort that do not cost money – various teaching techniques which can be especially useful in small groups. It's well worth bearing these points in mind.

The importance of movement. Not necessarily movement around the room (though this can sometimes be helpful!), but a nice 'pace' in the study – fairly rapid movement from slot to slot in your time-plan (which may of course relate to the various sections of the passage), so that people feel they are making progress in a logical and 'managed' way.

The art of directive questioning. One of the recent books on group Bible study, *Transforming Bible Study* by Walter Wink (Mowbray, 1990), emphasizes the creative power of a well-judged question, You know what you want the group to discover. You use a question like a crow-bar, to prize open the meaning of the passage for the group, or its significance for them. Some of your own 'why' (or other) questions may come into their own here. This is why, in the *Crossway Bible Guides*, we have usually provided questions rather than suggestions for study or activities: we hope they are questions of this sort, *directive* questions which first help you, and then can be used with the group if appropriate.

The stimulus of buzz-groups. It can be helpful to fire questions not at the group as a whole, but at small groups within it: divide them into twos or threes, and give them each a different question (or the same one) and four minutes to answer it. Then pool ideas. Provide 'clues' to the answer if appropriate. Using buzz-groups can give confidence to the shy members.

The involvement of a study guide. You may not have the time or resources to produce one, but a written study guide, with spaces for people to write answers or comments, can be very helpful. You can use it to provide essential background information in written form, which will be more effective than just speaking it to them. If people are working through a passage with a study guide, they are discovering for themselves, and if they are writing things down then they will remember better – especially if they are building up a course file week by week. Having materials like this makes it possible to review previous weeks easily, and to gain a sense of the way a whole book of the Bible fits together – something quite hard to achieve when a week elapses between each study. If you haven't got the time to produce study guides, your minister should be encouraged to do it! They are so valuable.

The provocation of a problem-solving approach. Why not try this teaching technique? It is the technique Jesus himself employs in the parables, which were his distinctive style of teaching (Mark 4:33–34). Rather than give people technical sermons about God and salvation he told a story. So people were immediately faced with the question, Why did Jesus tell this story? (Another 'why'!) They had to answer the question for *themselves* – he did not tell them either why he had chosen that particular story, or what it meant. His disciples got together afterwards for discussion – they were provoked and wanted to know what the parables meant (Mark 4:10).

Making up parables is extremely difficult. Have you ever

tried? Jesus' parables are so brilliant, and in themselves attest to his wonderful wisdom as the Son of God. But the *teaching technique* which underlies them is available to us all: you point to something odd or inexplicable, or you pose a practical problem, set a 'Christian life' case study, tease people with an apparent contradiction in the Bible, raise some topical issue from the news – and *get the group to discover* how the message of the passage solves or addresses it. Thus they *find for themselves* its vital relevance and power.

The clarity of visual presentation and reinforcement. A flip-chart or overhead projector can be very useful, simply because we live in a visually-oriented society and people more readily absorb *what they see*. These can be used in many ways, of course, during the session. But it will probably always be important for you as leader to give a visual summary, at the end of the session, of what you have all learned. You could write it on a slip of paper for people to keep in their Bibles until next week. Or you can attach a message to a symbol, like the shoe-lace in my Bible which reminds me of the Spring Harvest session at which we committed ourselves to support mission worldwide. Or you could put a sheet of paper on the floor and hand the pen to someone else – or pass a sheet round the group while they pray, ask them each to write what they have learned, and then read out the result. Whatever you do, you are employing the educational technique of *reinforcing learning*. People leave with their minds and hearts full of what God has taught them that day.

The creativity of learning through doing. This is something very strongly emphasized by Walter Wink in the book mentioned above. He reminds study-group leaders that our brains have right and left sides: the right side is oriented towards facts, words, analysis and logical thought, and is the side traditionally emphasized in Bible study. The left side deals with imagination, instinct, feelings, music, and non-verbal reasoning, and is traditionally ignored in Bible study. But Wink reminds us that we are not divided people: often we will be led to new insights into the meaning of the Scriptures as we bring *all* the resources of our minds to study them.

Wink suggests some very un-traditional activities to stimulate the engagement of the left-brain in Bible study. His book illustrates vividly the importance of careful leadership here, because some of the things he suggests would seem very strange indeed to British Christians! But the basic principle is sound, I believe, and fits with what we saw above about the way in which Paul holds together teaching, encouragement, and worship. To turn thoughts *into* some other medium – into music, drama, a parable, a role-play or other drama or symbolic action – this involves the creative engagement of the whole of our thinking and feeling nature. Paul especially mentions *singing*, and I must say that I personally find music one of the most powerful ways of sensing and appropriating Scriptural truth for myself.

The inspiration of example. Perhaps this is the most important resource of all – yourself. Your group looks to you not just to occupy that hour for them, but to *model to them the response for which the passage calls.* They need to see an example in you! And your leadership will *only* be effective if they see that example. Go for it!

The vital skills – *techniques of flexible direction*

Not much needs to be added here, because there is much relevant material in the rest of this book. But it is important to add that, having laid all your plans, focused your aim, formulated your questions, mapped out your time-allocations and decided your activities, it is vital to be flexible and to be ready to adjust it all in the light of what actually happens at the group. For instance, someone comes burdened with a particular need to share with the group. Rather than postpone the sharing to the end of the study, you see an opportunity to turn it into a teaching medium: what advice should we give? What do the Scriptures teach? What does this passage have to say about needs like this?

God will give you wisdom in this, and the wisdom will grow with experience. We need to capitalize on the unexpected, and not be thrown by it. Steering a discussion can be very difficult, and sometimes you will not be able to avoid aborting your aims! So it is great to be confident in God, and not in any collection of techniques or study-plans: he, after all, must be the teacher, or we learn nothing.

Finally, be encouraged! Teaching a small group is challenging, but very rewarding as you see your own gifts and skills developing through experience. The more you do it, the more effective you will become – and the more blessing you will see in the lives of the people you serve. 'Perfect love drives out fear', says John (1 John 4:18). Loving the group (and of course the Lord) will make the whole exercise a delight, and not a burden.

Chris Bowater is a member of the leadership team of New Life Christian Fellowship, Lincoln. A former school teacher he now travels widely (France and Portugal are presently a priority), leading worship conferences and developing a new generation of church musicians. Chris has written two books and hundreds of songs and recorded ten albums.
He is married to Lesley and their five children, his youngest (16) being triplets. Chris enjoys all sports from his armchair and the whole family supports Aston Villa football club. For holidays he prefers to get away from it all but they all tend to go with him!

Creative worship

Chris Bowater

There's no place like home

It is almost impossible to define exactly what worship is. Certainly it is more than the interminable singing of songs that typifies so many of our corporate worship times. Sadly, worship has become almost solely a musical activity, when in fact there is so much more, involving indeed our whole life-style. Worship must always be a vibrant, multi-dynamic expression of adoration, awe and thankfulness. The creator of all things deserves more than a song or two, a medley of thematically linked choruses! In reality, worship does not enrich God; telling him that he is great cannot make him greater, but it can enrich *us*. Therefore our corporate worship experience needs to be fortified with the enrichment of real people expressing the reality of their lives to a real God.

So often, when it comes to small-group worship the tendency is to reproduce large celebration-style meetings. The intensity of time and passion that large celebrations can justifiably generate is almost impossible to sustain in cell-group worship. All too easily the people become discouraged as the not too proficient guitarist grinds the worship into the carpet. The group become lost, in wonder, love and exhaustion! Far too easily the members move from being willing participators to embarrassed spectators.

'Spectatorism' is the antithesis of true praise and worship. Remember, you're at home, not in a cathedral, the Albert Hall or Spring Harvest. It should be a place where the group members can feel 'at home', be natural, be themselves.

Perhaps normal church life does not encourage that dynamic. Is it possible we have become more concerned with putting on a programme, fulfilling our ministries, than being concerned about real people who live in a very real world; like a football coach, more interested in the game-plan than with the players on the field? Housegroups give a marvellous opportunity to discover the rich contributions that can come from people whose perspectives have been honed by the rough hands of experience that nevertheless still bring praise and honour to God. Often the very close proximity of other people's lives deepens our understanding of God and his ways as they are allowed to express their preferences, feelings and expectations. In seeing the best and worst in each other God's grace has an opportunity to be operative in our lives. We learn together the ways of forgiveness, patience, thankfulness and mercy. Love becomes an action.

There is something very intimate and real about worship with and in front of a small group of people whom you have come to know and trust. You are forced to check the authenticity of your heart and your words, because they know you. One of the great benefits of intentionally taking the time, and having the courage, to be part of a small group is that you worship with people whom you know and care about. This does not sound like your housegroup? Perhaps careful maintenance of superficial relationships is producing a group of strangers. Perhaps there is good Bible study and ministry work but we still cover up our weaknesses and our real lives. We share about safe things rather than real things. *Koinonia* – intimate fellowship among Christians – seldom just happens. It takes time and hard work. It takes people who want to do the nitty-gritty work of developing a community of Christian friends.

Welcome!

It takes more than a cup of tea to make someone feel welcome, though it helps. The atmosphere of the home, the disposition of the leader and the other members are crucial to helping the reserved and the reluctant to relax. A suitable CD playing goes a long way to covering embarrassed silence. Family photo albums encourage natural conversations and young children in the home always seem to bring life and lightness into the room since they haven't yet learned to be religious. Perhaps we become preoccupied with starting a 'meeting' when in reality the greatest obstacle is simply to get people to meet.

As we understand that our corporate worship experience is more than singing songs, we will discover that everything we do can be meaningful worship. Let the time together be filled with encouragement. Leadership style is of great significance here. Determine that, as well as information given, there will be opportunities for personal insight to be shared. Here is where so often the proceedings grind to a halt. I have discovered that many people in church life neither expect nor are used to being involved. A deep lack of self-worth can lurk behind even the most gregarious mask. Everyone wants to be wanted, to have a sense of value. People who feel worthless among fellow Christians will also carry a strong sense of non-acceptance when it comes to God. Human and spiritual affirmation takes time and care. We must teach by word and example the value God places on each of us. This is foundational to a release of worship that is real and meaningful.

Small-group worship experience (1)

Some suggestions for the group leader

The following material, a short outline on the Song of Songs (Solomon) chapter 4:1–16, can work simply by being read to the group, but a more relaxed approach would be to use the information as a catalyst for personal involvement. Perhaps one member should read the verses, as appropriate, the leader, using his/her own words, relate the comments and others be invited to join in to discuss where it seems best.

Idea As an ice-breaker, equip everyone with pen and paper and ask the group to describe in words another person in the room. Invite the group to identify the person from the description.

Idea Similar to above, but this time the group members describe themselves, featuring physical and personality information as well as likes and dislikes. Again, spend time for the group to make the identification.

Dr Martyn Lloyd-Jones has said concerning the Song of Songs: 'It is a mine of spiritual treasure. It is one of the most exquisite expositions of the relationship of a believer and his Lord to be found anywhere in Scripture.' (N.B. he views this book as being a 'type' of the relationship between Jesus, the Bridegroom, and the church, his Bride, where other commentators see it as a human love song.) Certainly it is a graphic account of passionate love, so much so that the Jews forbade anyone to read this book until he was thirty years old!
Verse 1: 'How beautiful you are, my darling!' Looking into the mirror each morning may produce either fits of laughter or induce moods of depression as the effects of time on the face and body are observed. Most of us, even on the best, optimism-drenched day, rarely view ourselves as beautiful. But God, looking through the eyes of love, sees beauty, someone to be cherished and valued. With a voice as tender as eternal love, he whispers 'my darling.'
Verses 2–5: 'Your teeth . . .' This is where it starts getting a bit personal. He starts at the top and works his way down – in intimate detail God expresses his delight. Many of us can barely cope with an 'I love you' when it comes from one of our own species, so to receive such ravishing affection from God takes some doing. Here God describes us 'in the pink'. Not dressed up

in our Sunday best. He does not need to be impressed or convinced, God is already a devout believer. He believes in you and me. Nothing we can say or do will change his mind or stop him. He is in love! He loves us as we really are.

Verse 7: '. . . there is no flaw in you'. Does God mean this? Surely he can see the confusion and doubt, disappointments and regrets, and . . . well? Well, yes and no. Of course he can see, and yes he does know, because, after all, he is God. But this is the miracle. The all-knowing, all-sufficient, all-powerful (and the rest) God has made a choice. He has chosen to see what has been made clean and forgiven. Theologians call this the doctrine of justification by faith. In normal language, in God's eyes, it is just as if we had never ever sinned. That can be difficult to take in, to understand. That is why it is accepted by faith, the truth is received just as we do a gift. This truth is a gift from God. You and I are welcome in his presence, so draw near in the confidence that he sees no reason to stay away. Thank him and as we receive continual cleansing for the state of our present lives, let us enjoy standing complete in his presence.

Pray/Sing: God of grace, I turn my face to you, I cannot hide
My nakedness, my shame, my guilt are all before your eyes,
Striving and all anguished dreams in rags lie at my feet,
And only grace provides a way for me to stand complete,
And your grace clothes me in righteousness,
And your mercy covers me in love,
Your life adorns and beautifies,
I stand complete in You.
(Chris Bowater, 1990 © Sovereign Lifestyle Music)

Verse 9: '. . . with one glance of your eyes'. Every time God catches us looking at him, he is deeply moved. That is the effect our loving worship has on him. He is filled with anticipation when he sees that we are approaching him. He not only welcomes us, he wills us to spend time with him. With adoration he looks at us waiting for that moment when eyes meet. God, so awesome, fearful in power and majesty, marvels and delights in the look of love from his beloved.

Meditate: Here in the presence of the great and awesome God,
Here in the presence of the holy one,
The only one,
Knowing not how best to bring adoring love,
To bow, to fall, to weep and then you whisper
Child draw near . . .
Here in the presence of the great and awesome God,
Majestic in His power yet full of grace,
I seek your face,
The passion in your eyes, searches deep inside,
Such shining love intensifies yet melts away my fear
. . . and I
Stand in the presence of the Lord . . .
I stand in the presence of the Lord . . .
I stand in the presence of the holy one . . .
I stand in the presence . . . of the Lord
(Chris Bowater, 1995 © Sovereign Lifestyle Music)

Verse 12: 'You are a garden locked up . . .' I love gardens. I hate gardening. The land behind my house is euphemistically called a garden. It would never win prizes for design, colour or content. It is perhaps more suitable for missionary training! I enjoy walking through the great parks found in cities but take greater pleasure in discovering the creativity and colour of a private garden. Here, a labour of love, years of careful attention can be viewed.

How often our walk with God is on the terms of giving him access to the public gardens of our lives. Content that he is seen to be with us in the carefully selected and prepared open forums, the public meetings and ministry, the vast gardens of the outer life. All the time he longs to have access to the private place, the secret garden. He knows that the worth of our public agendas is always in relation to the openness of the hidden life. What we are at home is what we really are. What we are in the secrets of our hearts and desires is what we really are. The master longs to be given entrance, not that he might criticize or condemn but that he might begin to renew and rebuild. More than that, he does not always want to share us with everyone else. He wants us to himself, to talk, to listen, to share or quite simply, just be there.

Pray/Sing:

To be in your presence,
To sit at your feet,
Where your love surrounds me,
And makes me complete . . .
To dwell in your presence,
Not rushing away,
To cherish each moment,
Here I would stay . . .
This is my desire . . . Lord
(Noel Richards, 1991 © Thankyou Music)

Verses 13–14: 'Your plants . . . choice fruits'. Here there are shoots and fruits all in one glance, a sense of the beginning of things and the finishing of things together at one time. From God's perspective as he walks through our 'well watered gardens', because he is Alpha and Omega he can look at what is only the shoot of a new plant and see the fruit of ultimate fulfilment. The master gardener is committed in such a way that, as does Magnus Magnusson, he says, 'I've started . . . so I'll finish!'

Meditate/Memorize: Philippians 1:6, '. . . being confident of this, that he who began a good work in you will carry it on to completion . . .'

Verse 16: '. . . Blow on my garden . . .' A garden is never immune to the seasons. Winter is as much a certainty as springtime, summer as autumn. Our secret gardens too will not escape the cold north wind of adversity as well as hopefully enjoying the uplifting reassurance of the warm south wind.

Christianity does not eliminate the threat of suffering or the pain of loss. The hazards of real life are also there for us to overcome. He who walks through our secret garden wants to do so irrespective of the season. As he dances through the array of springtime splendour let him bring the cool of his peace in summer's heat. As the autumn garden glows with colour and a feast of precious memories slowly slip into the mists of uncertainty, allow him to be the 'I am . . .', the one who never leaves you, even when the winter freeze seems to kill off all hope. Remember, there always will be another springtime.

Each year, I look into that wasteland I call my garden and wish I could see some daffodils. Then I remember, I did not plant any!

Meditation: Lord, help me to make the effort to plant things that are worthwhile:

- In my own secret garden
- In my marriage
- In my family and friends

. . . because Lord, I do want to see some daffodils!

Activity: Allow time, perhaps with some meditative instrumental CD softly playing, for group members to write about their own secret garden. Invite them to be honest as they recognize the current season of their lives. I have found that this exercise can have a profound effect on people. Some people have written:

- 'Lord, I am a leader but where is my secret garden? I only know you in the public place . . .'
- 'Summer time should be so full of joy but God, I cannot cope with the heat of circumstances. I am tired of never-ending pressures . . .'
- 'So much of my life is behind me, time is running too fast.'

Remember to explain that this is not a competition. There is no need to try and impress. For those with literacy problems, a single phrase might be all that is needed.

Give the group the title: 'Lord, come and walk in my garden.'

Allow plenty of time and space . . . then gently invite people to enter a deeper level of group membership, vulnerability. Some will freeze. Do not force your way into these special moments. I have seen whole groups of people melt as vulnerable worship is read out. Support and affirm at all times. These can be deeply reverential and life bonding moments.

Small-group worship experience (2)

Let's turn to the song book (the Psalms and hints on how to use them)

The Psalms continue to live and grip the attention of needy humanity. Fads blossom and wilt, generations come and go, civilizations rise and fall, but the Psalms continue to survive the ages. No other book has been so fondly read and so freely commented on. The inescapable conclusion is – it has something helpful for us in every circumstance of life.

Psalms is a stupendous and marvellous book, enormous in teaching, amazing in faith, astonishing in trust and astounding in relevance. It covers the whole scope of living: everything that accompanies the far-flung and eventful life of mankind. Its extensive, up-to-date thoughts testify that we have always had to face the same problems. How little we change through the ages! As we read the Psalms, we realize that – with slight variations of circumstances – the author could be speaking of us this very hour.

The Psalms put into words all the questions, thoughts and feelings a believer could experience with his walk with God. There isn't a situation you can ever find yourself in, not an emotion you can think of, that isn't expressed in the Psalms in some form or other.

This marvellous book puts into human terms the reality of our relationship with God like no other book in the Bible. It expresses what it's like to know God and walk with him. No other portion of Scripture gives us such clear examples of ways in which we can pray and worship the Lord, and how we can express ourselves to the Father.

In essence, the Psalms is a book of prayer, praise and meditation. The Psalms teach us how to praise, what to thank God for and how to do it. They show what it means 'to pour out our hearts before the Lord,' by recording what David and other men of God said when they did so.

The Psalms is not so much a teaching book, as it is a worship book. To be sure, we can and should study the Psalms objectively to understand what is being communicated. But this study should be for the purpose of learning how to use the Psalms in the way they were intended to be used. They were written as an aid to prayer, worship and meditation (personal or corporate). Most benefit will be derived from them when we use them in this way.

Meditation on Psalm 145

1. Making the decision to praise (read Psalm 145:1–9).
2. Praising God's greatness (read Psalm 145:3–6, 10–13):
   - His mighty deeds
   - His glorious majesty.
3. Praising God's goodness (read Psalm 145:7–9, 14–21):
   - He is good to all
   - He is near to those who call.

Points for discussion

1. Why does true praise always involve a decision of our will? What do we do on those days when we do not feel like praising?
2. What are some of the ways we can make God's praise glorious in our private devotions? In corporate times of worship?
3. Have you ever seen something in God's creative work that caused you to respond in praise? What happened?

4. How has understanding God's greatness helped you better to appreciate his goodness?
5. What are some of the ways in which God is good to everyone? Why is this such a testimony to his great mercy? What are some of the particular ways that he is good to his own people?
6. What have you learned from this psalm that you can apply practically to your own life?

Activities after discussion (some ideas)

1. Invite the group to write their own psalms about how God is good to them as individuals.
2. Invite some of the group to share their psalms with the rest.
3. Accompanied by a single chord lead the group in singing their psalms – almost in chant style. If you do this all at the same time it should remove embarrassment (in theory!).
4. Do a similar exercise using Psalm 145:
   - all at the same time
   - taking turns to sing a verse.
5. Research all the songs sung at your church that come from, directly or indirectly, Psalm 145.
5. Sing them!
7. Use Psalm 145 as a guide to prayer, praise and meditation.

Worship in the round

Small groups offer a wonderful opportunity for worship. It's worship in a circle rather than in rows. It's worship where everyone can be a leader rather than just a select few. It's worship without preference. Rather than the complexity of bands, singers and sound systems this is worship with intimate friends.

Dangerously, church can become a place when only the professionals, the experts, have the opportunity to function. Housegroup is to be a place of reality, risk and fun.

Consider the neighbours!

Few of us live in palatial surroundings and in the world of the semi-detached house due consideration must be given to noise control.

- Use acoustic instruments (guitar, omni-chord, flutes, piano). The housegroup might not be the best platform for budding Hank Marvins.
- Keep it simple. This is not a concert.
- Choose songs that are easy to sing. This is an armchair environment not an auditorium. Choose songs that are easily sung sitting down (to stand to sing in someone's lounge seems to be totally bizarre).
- Select the best key. Usually a lower key is best suited to indoor, relaxed singing.
- Know your group. Each age group usually has its own preferences. Housegroup is all about learning to be gracious about someone else's preference.
- Most contemporary songs are easy to learn and remember but do not assume that everyone knows the song. A simple song sheet gives security to the more timid members.
- Involve the group in song selection. Do not be afraid of singing without instruments in the event of a song being chosen for which you do not have the music.
- Maintain a sense of humour. This is housegroup, not the church choral society. You will discover many and differing vocal 'gifts' in the vulnerability of housegroup worship.
- There might also be a place for using the growing number of backing tapes available. This does bring a quality control but can be very inflexible.

It is good to sing together. The Bible clearly is full of exhortations to sing. Remember though, worship is much more than song. Always encourage the ingredients of prayer, intercession, praise and worship, and meditation, at all times seeking for whole-group participation.

The small group and the open church

Enrich your times together with a broad range of activities. There is a universal human tendency to settle into a rut, doing the same types of things month after month. Whether it is worship and praise or fellowship and sharing, your meetings can easily drift into a sameness of form. You can add a great deal of depth by showing people how to inject a variety of contributions.

- Read Scripture aloud – normally with a reason for why you're reading it (don't make them guess!).
- Pray, being sure to include, over the months, all types and topics of prayer: individual, group, praise/worship, petition, repentance, sentence prayers, conversational prayers, and lots of thanksgiving.
- Testify! Give a report of God's grace in your life recently. Recount a story of something you saw or heard or experienced, a story that teaches a spiritual truth or a fact about God.
- Prophesy. Prophecy is, at root, an especially acute insight into the mind of God on some subject or event. It does not have to involve prediction. It does involve listening carefully to God and then telling others what he has said.
- Meditate/Reflect on what the last person just said.
- Celebrate communion together when possible, according to your church tradition, and involve everyone, take turns in leading. If the administration of the bread and wine can only be performed by an ordained minister, seek other ways of group involvement, especially in sharing 'the peace'.
- Preach! It does not have to be a full-course sermon. Three minutes will do just fine.
- Reinforce! When someone says something that resonates with your spirit, back him or her up with a brief response, a word of agreement, or even a brief elaboration of the point. Everyone needs affirmation and you'll build unity that will last like the pyramids.

- Take notes!
- Get physical! Don't go way beyond the norm for your group and embarrass people, but loosen up and become more tactile. Try things like holding hands to pray as an expression of togetherness, laying on hands (in the biblical sense) if someone needs extra-special prayer, clapping, raising hands, kneeling . . . but don't ever let it become unreal. Sincerity and reverence must always exist but always as an expression of love and life.
- Lead a song, a hymn, a round, a chorus. Divide the group and sing antiphonal songs (men/women, left/right, adults/kids).
- Sing a song yourself – or devise a duet/trio, *etc*.
- If you're not up to any of the above – ask for help!

Often, housegroup members need the security of time to prepare special contributions. Everyone is not comfortable in an environment of spontaneity. Think and plan ahead.

In the early church, there was not always a pre-set order of worship. Contributions were probably mostly spontaneous, as the Spirit led. In a typical congregation, there was often no single speaker who always spoke. On the other hand, there were no pure spectators, either. Everyone was encouraged to take part. Shyness is always an understandable factor but let any silence be a positive involvement of listening and meditating. Everyone has something of value to share.

Enjoy one of the greatest pleasures, you and others being an active and valued part of the Body of Christ.

Enjoy!

Jon Bush is part of the ministry team at Mutley Baptist Church in Plymouth. Over the past fifteen years he has served in various churches, including First Baptist Church Dallas, Westminster Chapel and Herne Bay Baptist Church. He has been overseeing housegroups and writing study material for them for the past ten years and is convinced that healthy housegroups are essential for fellowship and spiritual growth in churches. He is married with two teenage sons and a younger daughter and enjoys fast food and holidays in America.

A trouble-shooter's guide

Jon Bush

How to spot and handle awkward people

The housegroup leader needs to spot awkward people in the group as early as possible. This is not because it is desirable to exclude them from the group or because other members need to be warned off them but it is important to be prepared. In this way if a difficult situation arises the leader will be ready to deal with it. Forewarned is forearmed!

The housegroup leader needs to pray in his/her own 'quiet time' for each member of the group by name. Ask God to give you the gift of knowledge. This is the ability to have godly insight into situations and people. 'Lord, enable me to see more deeply than what is discernible naturally.'[1] You need insight not only into what people are like but also into understanding why they are like it. Try to meet their families and other friends and try to understand and appreciate their personal circumstances.

Non-verbal language

Watch each member of the group even before the prayer, study or worship time begins. Look for unnatural signs of coolness or awkwardness. Where do people sit? Do some people always choose a particular seat, not for its comfort but because of where it is in relation to the rest of the group? Does their chair become either a vantage point from which they attack others or a cave in which they take refuge?

Be aware of body language. This is a complex subject but it is important. Research suggests that we actually communicate much more by non-verbal signs than verbally.[2] How someone walks may convey expectancy or heaviness. Appropriate touching conveys affection, warmth and trust. Good eye contact suggests understanding and acceptance. A relaxed posture without folded arms or crossed legs suggests openness. Look out for what people communicate even before they speak.

The dominant member

When it comes to time for comment, sharing or discussion, listen not only to what is said but to how it is said. Are some people more interested in the response they evoke from others than in sharing so that others may be enlightened or blessed? Are they willing to listen to other people? How do they handle disagreement? Do they want to dominate the group completely or to turn the conversation to their pet hobby horse? Problems in one or more of these areas do not necessarily mean that you have an awkward person on your hands but they may warn of difficulties ahead.

It is always best to deal with unhelpful comments and attitudes when they occur. Certainly the leader should aim to do this at the first or second 'offence'. Loving and constructive confrontation can actually be a spiritually strengthening and maturing factor in the life of the group (Ephesians 4:15). If a person or a group of people persist in behaving badly it is appropriate to tackle them outside the housegroup setting, possibly involving a member of the church leadership (Matthew 18:15–17; Titus 3:10). In extreme cases the biblical directives may need to be applied.

Most groups have at least one member who is inclined to take over and dominate times of discussion. Tackle these types of people on two fronts. By limiting them: 'Mike, you have had a good say' or, 'Ruth, you have made a number of points' and by drawing in other people to speak: 'Let's hear from someone else now' or, 'Someone else give us a perspective on that'. I know one housegroup leader who has a very talkative person in her group whose contribution is valuable but who tends to swamp and silence other people. The leader has a good relationship with him and will often follow a question to the group with a big smile towards her talkative member and the comment: 'Anyone may answer except . . .' Later she gives him an opportunity to speak.

The quiet member

At the other extreme are the silent and retiring people who make little or no verbal contribution to the group either in discussion, prayer or even in the chat over coffee afterwards. The leader needs to pray and ask God to give insight into what lies behind this reticence. It may be that these are genuinely quiet, gentle people who, whatever the setting, would have little to say. There is nothing wrong with this and you need not regard these people as 'problems'. Their silence does not mean that they are not 'with' the group and supportive of it. However, the leader may feel that it is right to try and draw them out by asking them to read a verse of Scripture (prepare for this in advance and make sure they are able to read) or answer a factual question rather than share feelings or opinions.

The problematic quiet person is the one who uses his silence as a way of showing contempt for the group. He wants to have an unsettling effect on people. He is usually an angry, hurt person who feels let down by others or even by God. He needs to be shown lots of unconditional love and acceptance by the whole group. Even when his anger does eventually burst out into hostile words the group needs to send him the message: 'We accept you and we love you.' The group leader needs to exercise a skilful role in encouraging the group to make such a response at the same time as protecting it from attitudes and words that may be harmful. Time spent by the housegroup leader alone with the person will probably be very helpful in integrating him into the group.

Another character who is often present in the housegroup is the apparently well-read type who constantly quotes other people. The leader should not be afraid to say to a person like that: 'What do *you* think?' This person is hiding behind what others say and lacks confidence in expressing his own thoughts. Generally, the leader should urge people to talk in the first person as this will make for a more relevant and meaningful discussion of God's word.

A light, humorous spirit is usually helpful in the group. Difficult and tense moments may often be defused by the appropriate use of humour. What is unhelpful though is when a member of the group makes everything into a joke or pokes fun at others in the group. Sometimes deep, special moments may be hijacked by a frivolous comment. People who behave like this may be trying to hide their true feelings or may want to attract attention to themselves. Recognizing this, the leader should do all that he can to draw attention away from these people by showing, in a friendly way, that he/she does not find this approach helpful. He may also address questions to the people concerned to try to bring them back to the issue under discussion.

The hostile member

Perhaps the most destructive kind of person in a group is the one who acts in a negative or hostile way towards others. Such people, for a variety of reasons, probably feel bad about themselves and project their anger and negativism on to others. This behaviour has the potential of making other people very unhappy and even of dividing the group. They must be confronted in a constructive way outside the group (Matthew 18:15–17; Titus 3:10). If the behaviour persists and unhelpful comments continue to be made it may become necessary during the housegroup meeting to ask: 'Do you realize how a comment like that hurts people in this room?' Be ready for some painful but constructive conversation to follow. An episode of this sort will be a real test as to the unity of the group which must continue to make this person feel welcome and accepted as part of the group.

Responding to the slowest and the quickest members of the group

The housegroup is not a neat, predictable machine. It is made up of people who differ from each other in a whole host of ways and whose words and responses are not always what you would expect. People vary in the pace at which they move in regard to their understanding of what is being taught in the group and their acceptance of where the group is going and what it is trying to achieve as a Christian community. Two important points need to be made on this subject. Firstly, growth in the Christian life is not an academic exercise. Secondly, we must not underestimate the role of the Holy Spirit in giving insight and understanding (1 Corinthians 12:1–11).

The slower members

It is important that the leader be aware of who is lagging behind the majority of the group and who is so far ahead that it is uncomfortable for everyone else. Some people are simply slow to pick up new and different ideas. They may be identified by the confused expression on their face or their questions and comments may reveal that they are actually where the group was the week before or two weeks ago. It is vitally important that these people are in no way put down or ridiculed by the rest of the group. The leader may have to fend off criticism from other members that they are holding the group back but hopefully those comments will never be aired publicly.

The whole group should be encouraged to be positive and supportive of the slower member, encouraging him to be more explorative and open in his thinking. It might be helpful to assign another member who already has a good relationship with this person, to raise the question informally over coffee or at some other time: 'How did you enjoy housegroup this evening?' or 'What do you feel you got out of the study tonight?' (This should not be done in a patronizing or critical way.) The conversation that arises may give the opportunity to clarify and reinforce the teaching that has been given.

What about the person who has no difficulty grasping what is being discussed and taught but is unwilling to move forward with the group in working out practically what is being learned from the Bible and in realizing the goal the group has set for itself? These people may be recognized by their general uneasiness or by their quietness at certain suggestions or their gentle or aggressive (depending on personality) verbal resistance to what is suggested.

At all costs a situation must be avoided where the rest of the group sets itself up against these people or in the end they will get the blame for anything that goes wrong in the group. Many people react in this way because they feel comfortable and secure with things just as they are. They would feel threatened and vulnerable if things were to change. The leader must recognize this and work with the group to create a sense of security and trust so that these people may feel that they are in safe hands. Then, although the group may do different things or go in a new direction, their security may be drawn from the group and not just from walking on familiar ground.

The quicker members

Those who are 'ahead' of the rest of the group will grasp ideas very quickly and arrive at their conclusions almost before other people have left the starting blocks of the discussion. It is easy to recognize people like this. Their general attitude may be one of impatience or even cynicism over other people's apparent slowness. They need to be encouraged, probably privately, to recognize that they are part of the group and that they should be constantly asking themselves: 'What will be good for and a blessing to those around me?' They need to be reassured that they are loved and valued for themselves and do not need to be ahead of everyone else in order to be thought highly of. In the group they may be handled by asking the question: 'How have you arrived at that conclusion?' This would get them to retrace their steps and would involve the rest of the group in asking if they could go along with that. However, this would not be a helpful pattern to follow at every meeting!

Change and stability

Some people thrive on change. They want it to be radical and they want it now! In a housegroup these kinds of people may well be heard saying: 'If we were doing this . . .' or 'The problem with this group is . . .' The focus of their frustration is often those in the group who appear cautious or enjoy things as they are. They may criticize the leader for not bringing about the change that they think is needed. Again they need to be encouraged to get the focus off themselves and to recognize that they are part of a community in which other people's needs and feelings must be considered.

However, there are times when a group does become too inward-looking and complacent. Whatever the reasons for this, it is time for the leadership of the church to take a careful look, with sensitive and pastoral eyes, at why this has happened. The group may need the input of others who will challenge its outlook. These new members and possibly a new leader will need to be mature and patient and be prepared to love and work with people who, for a variety of reasons find change difficult and threatening. Sadly, some people may leave the group because they find the new way of doing things too costly.

There is always the temptation with housegroups to bring together in one group like-minded people who are moving at the same pace, be that slowly or quickly. Inevitably there will be a natural coming together of people who feel comfortable with each other but to do this in an organized way should be avoided. The value and richness of the group's life and the individual's own spiritual growth will come, in part, out of coping with and loving people who think differently.

Leading the housegroup forward

A housegroup is a living body because it is made up of human beings. Like the church, there is no housegroup where there are no people. As with anything that is living, the housegroup will change over a period of time. There will be good times and times when it is hard going. There will be times of numerical growth and times of low attendance. The group will feel at times that it is going somewhere and at others that very little progress is being made. These ups and downs may be caused by people leaving the group or joining it, by what is going on in the wider life of the church, by periods of change or stress in individual lives or by what is being studied and discussed by the group. The housegroup leader will soon be disappointed if he expects it always to be a 'third heaven' experience at the group's meetings.

Purpose of the group

Competent leadership together with a clear understanding of the purpose and aim of the group is crucial in leading the housegroup forward.

Leadership is not only about an able and well-prepared housegroup leader who sees through the actual housegroup meeting and gives overall direction to the group. It is also about a host who welcomes people into his home. It is about having someone to oversee all the administrative and secretarial aspects related to the group. It is about making sure that the group's pastoral needs are responded to or passed on to the appropriate leader in the church and that prayer is encouraged for and by the group. Competent leadership must embrace all these aspects though not necessarily in only one person. Ideally there should be a committed and closely knit team. Such a team will need to meet together to pray and talk about the life and direction of the group.

However, a good leadership team should not create an 'us and them' situation regarding the rest of the group. Every person attending the group should have a sense of being a part of it and of being behind what it is trying to achieve. This is relatively easy when people attend regularly and are by nature supportive and encouraging. It is more difficult with members who attend spasmodically or with those who are naturally critical and easily find fault.

Content of the meetings

The content of the study material may be decided on independently of the housegroup by the church leaders (hopefully in consultation with the housegroup leaders) but if each group decides on its own material, make sure that the group is consulted on its views before the leader finally decides what is to be studied. The content of the material may not be popular with everyone. It may even be used as an excuse for someone to leave the group permanently or to stop coming for a time. Others may remain present but respond to what is taught in a negative or obstructive way.

It may be that when the group is planning an evangelistic evening or is preparing to lead a church service or take a prayer meeting some people will question whether they have a role to play in this or will dissociate themselves from the group. In personal conversation the housegroup leader should try to ascertain why the person has reacted in this way and emphasize the 'family' nature of the group: 'We are a family of people who differ from each other in many ways. Not everything is going to appeal to everybody in the same way. Stay involved for the enriching of your own experience and in order to support and encourage people for whom this series of studies or activity is a particular help and blessing.'

Finding individual gifts

In my experience, even in the same church, housegroups vary a lot in their outlook and style of operation. When people say they want to attend a housegroup I encourage them to try two or three and find which one suits them best. (I always hope they will choose the one nearest to where they live.) People change, housegroups change, and it may be that after someone has attended one group for a number of years he may feel more at home in another group. It is important to ask why he is making the change. It would be wrong for him to be 'running away' from any person or situation in his previous group.

Greater 'ownership' of the group by its members will be achieved when they feel that they have a part in making decisions concerning the material to be studied and what the group does and how it does it. People's commitment to the group will be increased when they are able to use their gifts or talents for the service of the group. The housegroup is an ideal environment for people to find and begin to exercise their spiritual gift (John 16:13). The encouragement and support they get from the group in this is crucial to their continuing use of the gift and to their perception of how much the group is 'with' them.

The birth of a new group

Once a housegroup has more than twelve people attending regularly it is probably too large. Ultimately the numbers that constitute too large a group will depend on the dynamics of the group, the leader's gifting and, on a practical level, the size of the room where they meet. The church leadership should anticipate splitting the group before it is actually necessary in order to sow the idea with the group at an early stage. Most groups love and appreciate their leader and when a split is proposed a common question is: 'Where is the leader going?' Separation from the paternal or maternal figure in the group will be made easier if a deputy leader has actively shared in leadership in the past and can now take on the leadership of either the old group or the new one.

It is always helpful if the new group is located in an area where some of the members live, making it natural for them to join this new group. The church leadership may also encourage certain people to move to the new group because they need a new challenge or because they have a special contribution to make there.

The split (this word has unfortunate connotations; we are really talking about the birth of a new group out of an existing one) ought to be advertised in the church and people who aren't already involved in a group should be encouraged to join at this point. People are much more inclined to come on board at a time of change and fresh starts than when things appear to be stable and fixed. Dividing a group needs to be handled sensitively and carefully. Nothing should be forced through and it should be begun in prayer among the church leadership long before it actually comes to fruition.

Evaluation

The vision and direction of a group must be determined in consultation with the leadership of the church who should set down at least a long-term vision for its housegroups for what they should become in time. It is probably desirable to leave the short-term vision or steps towards the big picture to the housegroups themselves, bearing in mind the unique nature of each group. From time to time a housegroup should meet to ask such questions as: Why do we exist? What do we want to achieve? What should we become? How can we achieve it? What must we change or do differently in order to realize our goal? Such discussion will be unwelcome to some who are wary of change. It should be entered into in as non-threatening a way as possible whilst making sure that anyone who finds what is being said or decided on hard to take feels valued and wanted in the group.

These reflective and forward-looking sessions should only take place for the whole group once or twice a year because they are unsettling for some people and can actually be a hindrance to getting on with the job of being a housegroup. The leader, and if appropriate the leadership team, should keep an eye on whether the group is navigating the agreed course. If change or new direction is decided upon it must be implemented. This is the point at which many 'church' decisions fail with the lion's share of time and energy being given to what must be done but with little thought as to how it is going to be achieved. Hopefully, some visionary talking and goal-setting will help to increase the sense of purpose in the group. It will also be a way of measuring whether progress is being made. Some decision-making will need to be done under the direction of or in consultation with the church leadership. It will only lead to confusion if housegroup members see that the church is going in one direction and their housegroup is going in another. Not asking questions about what direction the group is going in might well lead to a cosy group but it will actually be achieving nothing for God's kingdom.

Pitfalls to avoid

I approach this subject with caution because I believe it is wrong to undertake housegroup leadership with the attitude that you are going to do everything possible to avoid disappointment or controversy. These things are always a part of people working together, even in the Christian community. Furthermore, it may well be in the less welcome aspects of leading a group, at times when you feel weak and vulnerable, that God is most able to be himself. However, we are still called to be as 'shrewd as snakes' (Matthew 10:16).

Avoid the following pitfalls.

1. Judging your worth as a person or as a Christian by how well the housegroup is doing. We should judge our worth purely on the basis of what God feels about us and what he has done for us.
2. Don't judge the 'health' of the group on your own 'performance'. Housegroup leaders are rightly too involved to judge how an evening has gone. I encourage housegroups to appoint a deputy housegroup leader, one of whose roles should be to keep a finger on the pulse of the group and to keep the leader informed as to how well he perceives things are going.
3. The leader will have been chosen and appointed by the

leadership of the church. He must not allow anyone else, regardless of how strong his personality is or how well he would do the job, to take over the leadership of the group.

4. Don't allow the group to become gossipy or critical or a pressure group against something or someone in the wider life of the church. If a leader sees this happening and cannot do anything to avert it he should draw in a member of the leadership of the church.

5. Don't become discouraged by reports of how big or how well other housegroups are doing. Every group is different. A housegroup leader's primary calling is to be faithful not successful.

6. As housegroup leader you may well become respected and trusted by the members of the group. Don't let this lead you into any unwise or compromising position with a member of the opposite sex.

7. Make sure that you do not attribute the success of the group to yourself. This is damaging for the morale of the group and robs God of his rightful honour.

How to keep sane!

Keep Christ at the centre of all you are doing. It is easy to put the group in the centre. You may focus in on a particularly needy person. It may seem right to study a theme or a passage of scripture and to say: 'This is what we are concerned with more than anything else.' At times, you will be tempted to put yourself in the centre. All these things have their place but, first and foremost, Jesus – loving, serving and following him – must be top of our agenda.

You need to have a sense of call to lead a housegroup. Your call and the necessary gifting and equipping which is part of it need to be recognized by the church's leadership when you are asked to take on a group and the group itself must be willing to accept your leadership. There may be times when you are criticized or feel hurt or overlooked. At times like this the only thing you can hold on to is the knowledge that God has called you to this task and until he rescinds that calling you must stick with the responsibility. Remember that you and your house-group are in God's hands. He is the leader. Don't take yourself too seriously and enjoy what you are doing.

Notes

1 David Pytches, *Spiritual Gifts in the Local Church* (Bethany House Publishers, 1985).
2 Findings by Mehrabian quoted by Paul D. Meier, Frank B. Minirth, Frank B. Wichern, Donald E. Ratcliff, *Introduction to Psychology and Counselling* (2nd ed. Monarch, 1991).

Dave Cave has spent twenty-one years church planting in the inner city. He spends time preaching and teaching in prisons, pubs, churches and theological colleges and appears on television and radio. His main concern is Christian ministry to the poor, not only conversion but justice and social issues. He is married to Tina. They have two sons in their twenties and enjoy relaxing on the British canal system, listening to music and keeping fish.

Communicating truth to today-people

Dave Cave

Methods of communication have changed significantly in the past thirty years. Take two examples – the news and music videos. At one time the news was a presentation of facts with in-depth discussion, now it's mainly quick news and headlines. Music videos have followed a similar framework. *Top of the Pops* has come a long way from the stand-up singer to the quick-flash images when the artiste changes clothes up to thirty times in one song!

So how do we study the Bible! How up to date are we with modern media methods of communication? How do we find effective ways of getting the message of the Good News of Jesus Christ across to an increasingly non-book culture? Even the people who can read are less inclined to do so than those of the last generation. My intention in this chapter is to attempt to answer some of those questions.

'Christ is the answer' proclaimed a large poster outside one local church building and I felt very tempted to get a felt-tip and write underneath, 'What was the question?' Graffiti books seem to be popular at the moment, and they all have their fair share of similar responses; 'Jesus saves . . . but Fowler gets it on the rebound'; 'Where will you be when the Lord returns? – still waiting for the 93 bus', and many more. But they all shout out one thing – the Christian community is failing to get across its message.

We must recognize that the language of our religious institutions is not the language of the council estate and the inner city, let alone the suburbs. The sermon is rarely delivered in the everyday language of the people.

When I first arrived at theological college there were all sorts of words flying around which completely bewildered me. Words like 'exegesis', 'parousia' and 'realized eschatology'. It frightened the life out of me and made me feel so ignorant that I really questioned whether I should be there at all. (By the way, I discovered later 'exegesis' was the explanation of Bible passages, 'parousia' was just another word for talking about Jesus returning, and 'realized eschatology' is Bible prophecies which have been fulfilled.)

Another example of this came from my own children when they were four and five years old. We got into the pattern of telling a story every night at bedtime and at that moment we were on the story of Moses and the Israelites in the wilderness. We got to the point where Moses brought water from the rock and my eldest son stopped me and asked,'Was it hot water or cold water?' 'I don't know, I suppose it was cold water.' 'Oh, if there had been two holes, one would have been hot water, and the other would have been cold.' This was a reasonable assumption as his experience of water was of two taps, one hot, one cold. It is very important for us as Christians to appreciate the cultural understanding and use of language.

Understanding language

How can we communicate the Good News of Jesus in a time and generation when words like 'God' and 'Christ' are just swear words, where the chances are that 'the person in the street' thinks that Leviticus is the name of a horse in the 2:30?

Maybe the first thing to realize is that language helps communities to identify. The book of Judges gives us a classic example of this: 'whenever a survivor of Ephraim who was trying to escape said, "Let me cross over," the men of Gilead asked him,

"Are you an Ephraimite?" If he replied, "No", they said, "All right, say 'Shibboleth'." If he said, "Sibboleth", because he could not pronounce the word correctly, they seized him and killed him at one of the fords of the Jordan' (Judges 12:5–6). The way you speak is important.

'Jesus is Lord' doesn't mean a lot in our area, in fact the word 'lord' is virtually extinct as far as local use is concerned. But a lot of local graffiti proclaim: 'Boot boys rule OK' or 'Liverpool rules OK' so to say 'Jesus rules OK' has a whole lot more force behind it – what you might call God's graffiti.

One thing which struck me when reading Paul's account of his own conversion was where he said, 'I heard a voice saying to me in Aramaic' (Acts 26:14). Jesus spoke to Paul in his mother tongue, although Paul was just as happy speaking Greek (Acts 21:28). Jesus, himself, felt it was important to speak to Paul on the Damascus road in the language of Paul's culture, in order to identify and so communicate with him much more effectively. It is not surprising to read that Paul uses the same approach and with some effect, 'When they heard him speak to them in Aramaic, they became very quiet'; and Paul went on: 'I am a Jew, born in Tarsus of Cilicia but brought up in this city.' (Acts 22:2–3); just a few moments before the same crowd had been screaming, 'Away with him!' (Acts 21:36).

Often, the most effective media for communication in today's society are the proverb, the chorus, the joke, the testimony, the miracle story, and the television and radio programme. The point being that it's easier to understand and remember a story than a verse or a sentence.

Notice that successful speakers who manage to bridge the culture communication gap rely quite heavily on stories and humour. Arthur Blessit of the Jesus Movement in California was very effective in speaking to people in the Black Panther movement, hell's angels, drug addicts, and prostitutes; what you might call today's version of the Biblical phrase 'publicans and sinners'; and his whole approach to sharing the Good News of Jesus was to tell one story after another. He came to speak in

Bradford while I was there and for three nights running St. George's Hall was packed, mainly with young people. They understood him and responded in larger numbers than to any other speaker I have witnessed. Would the tax collectors and the outcasts have joined Jesus and his disciples and listened to his teachings if he had confined himself to quoting chunks of Scripture without putting it into a form that they could understand and absorb?

People can only respond to a truth mentally; that is, they can either accept it or reject it, whereas a story also gives you an opportunity to react emotionally. Nathan made great use of this principle in getting King David to see where he had gone wrong when he had Bathsheba's husband, Uriah, killed so that he could avoid the issues involved in the fact that he (David) had made Bathsheba pregnant (2 Samuel 1:27). First Nathan tells the story of a rich man, with many cattle and sheep, taking a poor man's pet lamb (2 Samuel 12:1–4). David responds to the story emotionally, 'David burned with anger against the man and said to Nathan, "As surely as the LORD lives, the man who did this deserves to die!" ' Then Nathan comes in with the punch-line, 'You are the man!' (2 Samuel 12:6–7).

In Bible studies it is better to avoid getting a leader to ask questions because there is a natural desire to want to please by giving 'the right answer'. Questions should usually be one-way, from the group to the leader. Better to allow people to draw their own conclusions from a story than try to build up knowledge on a question-and-answer pattern. It may well be that a story means one thing to one group in one situation and something else, very different, but just as relevant, in another place at another time.

Take, for instance, the story of Jesus walking on the water (Matthew 14:22–32). Any number of deeper meanings can be drawn from it.

- If you really trust Jesus you can walk on water.
- We can try to live the Christian life in our own strength but

we will always fail and so we need Jesus to 'pull us out' – especially in a fight.

- Peter fell in because pride started to get a hold on him and it's the same with us. Every time we start thinking we're doing it, instead of God doing it, we get in a mess.
- I can give up drugs/alcohol/tobacco as long as I keep my eyes on Jesus and trust him.

All four meanings could be taken from that story by the young people in our fellowship, but it would depend on the situation they were in as to which was the most relevant at any one time.

Use of language is constantly changing – when you hear the word 'bizzy' in Liverpool today it means a policeman. Yet thirty years ago the word didn't exist and policemen were then referred to as 'scuffers'. The same is also true for religious language and the result is that many words now have no more meaning than the word 'scuffer'. So when we sing about 'raising Ebenezers' and seeing 'bright Shekinah clouds' what are we communicating?

The language of the Good News of Jesus must move with the time and the place at which it is being shared. If we are not careful we can develop a form of religious language which, like much church architecture, can become frozen theology: you can tell the generation in which it was developed.

In order to try and understand some of the issues relating to the non-book culture of today it may be helpful to examine my 'Ten Commandments' in relation to communicating the Good News of Jesus Christ.

1. Don't assume that people read books

The majority of people today read a tabloid newspaper such as the *Daily Mirror*, if they read at all. If you look at something like the *Daily Mirror*, most of it consists of big headlines, not thousands of words on one page but a small amount of words on a page (usually using simple vocabulary), lots of pictures and cartoons. Most people will rarely read it all, they will look at the headlines, maybe the TV page, the sports page, the cartoons, the advertisements, but not all of them.

Many folk cannot cope with small print such as tax forms, and many a time they have to go to other people to help them to work through social security forms *etc.* because they don't know where to begin in understanding them. Even people who can read get 'word blindness' when there are too many words close together in small print as in some Bibles.

2. Teach groups or gangs, not individuals

We have a habit of picking-off the weakest in the community and getting through to them. For instance, in a council-housing estate the church tends to target the children first, then the mothers and only afterwards the fathers.

The power of peer-group pressure is strong in that kind of culture. So what is taught a child in half an hour in church on a Sunday is easily dismissed by peer-group pressure or from parents during the week. So if you are going to make an impact you go to the identifiable groups, whether it is a street gang, a young mums' group or somebody that meets in the launderette, or a gang of fellows that are down at the pub.

The example I give is Dave Wilkerson's experiences described in his book *The Cross and the Switchblade* (Lakeland Publishers, 1964). Recognize what he was doing under the guidance of the Spirit of God in trying to bring gangs to Christ. He didn't go for the weak characters, he went for the jugular you might say, because he went for the toughest of the leaders of the gang, knowing that if he got through to him, he had an opportunity to get through to the rest of the gang. That's how he made his impact and that's what we need to do in communicating into the situation.

If we try and impose our standards and our approach to communication using the Bible and the Good News on our terms, working only with those individuals who are usually the weakest, we will fail. Most people who respond to Christians on their own will revert immediately they are back in their peer group.

3. Don't meet in church buildings but on their territory

If a person is looking for help it is unusual for them to go to a church building. It is much more normal for them to go to someone's home, usually a person that they know.

If we are going to communicate we tend to communicate where we feel secure, and where we have our institutions. And it frightens the life out of a lot of people – I have heard of people going to certain churches where they are handed a prayer book and then they are handed a hymn book and a book of choruses, and possibly the latest *Series* service. They have so many books that they just panic and they put the whole lot down and go. When they are already on foreign territory (church buildings), it's totally threatening.

Church buildings are not often warm, friendly and inviting; in the inner-city they are often like fortresses in the middle of housing estates. Only when the buildings are used for other activities than worship is the local community likely to have any identity with the building.

The challenge to us is to go where the people are and to communicate with them. You have to learn to talk it through and to communicate it through in a totally different way from the way we are used to. It may be someone's house, in the bar of the local pub, in the supermarket or at the bus stop. We need to use an unchurchified approach.

4. Mind your language

There was a lad from our Fellowship, Buster, a local drug addict and drug pusher, who could hardly read and write. He came into the Fellowship fresh from the streets. One classic quote puzzled him: 'Take my yoke upon you for my burden is light'. I discovered some months afterwards that Buster thought that this meant smashing an egg over your head because that was his only experience of a yoke (yolk!).

At Caesarea Philippi Jesus said, ' "Who do people say the Son of Man is?" Peter answered, "You are the Christ, the Son of the living God." ' (Matthew 16:13, 16). One suggestion of how this question might be answered by a clergyman today says, 'You are the eschatological manifestation of the ground of our being, the charisma that exists in all interpersonal relationships.'

Too much of our Christian message is wrapped up in jargon: 'Are you washed in the blood?', 'Touched by the loadstone of Thy love', 'The hill of Zion yields a thousand sacred sweets', 'Holy anointed One'. These are all lines from some of the hymns we sing which convey nothing to the non-believer. Have you considered how much of the language that you and I use in church is not used in the community? It would be interesting to take a number of words like 'sanctification', 'redemption' and 'holiness' and ask folk to attempt to explain them in your Bible study and see who understands them.

The Bible says, 'If anyone speaks in a tongue, two – or at the most three – should speak, one at a time, and someone must interpret' (1 Corinthians 14:27). Someone must interpret because we actually do speak in tongues. Paul would have had in mind the situation in the synagogue where one of the officers had the job of interpreting from the Hebrew into the local language as not everyone spoke Hebrew (Acts 6:1). We need to be sensitive to the use of language, making sure we speak in a way that local people can understand. The Good News is wonderful, the Good News is powerful, but if it's locked up in a kind of language that people don't understand then what hope is there?

5. Work on a supply and demand basis

Don't tell them more than they want to know. As Bible study leaders we feel, 'I have prepared all this and I'm going to tell you it all whether you want to know or not', instead of attempting to respond to people's needs where they are at that moment.

If I can give you a simple illustration. I have two sons who are now bigger than I am, but when they were little they started asking questions about where babies come from. I remember when they were about four or five my sons came and said, 'Dad, where do babies come from?' and I said, 'Well, from your mum's tummy.' That's all they wanted to know and they toddled off quite happy. I could have gone into all sorts of gynaecological and fertilization lectures but it would have gone totally over their heads. It would have been a total waste of time.

Then a bit later they came back with another question, 'Dad, How do the babies get in mum's tummy?' So I thought about this and I thought deep theological thoughts and I said, 'Go and ask your mum.'!

The point I am making is that we should make more of an effort to answer people's questions rather than giving them answers that they are not ready for. Education in the University of Life follows that pattern – children grow up asking questions expecting simple answers, usually from their parents. We have got to learn that as Christians it is supply and demand. Don't go forcing the Good News down people's throats. Wait until they are hungry and then you'll find yourself much more effective.

6. Learn to use audio-visual aids

This is hard work because it's not the way that we are conditioned to respond. We are conditioned to be an audience with an entertainer or a teacher with a class. That's the way that it operates in church circles but that is not the way of the culture that I come from and people just do not handle it. So ask yourself, how do most people communicate in a culture where the majority of people do not own books, apart from the rent book and the catalogue?

It's an interesting observation for me that in working-class Anfield where I lived for many years there are more video shops than in the middle-class areas. Many more people today have so much time on their hands, and they live their lives out through *Neighbours*, *Coronation Street* and *Brookside* – they will watch everything and anything on the telly because it's visual, but switch off when they are talked at.

Many folk today are visual people, they absorb more information through pictures rather than through academic ideas. It is vital that Christians make the effort to develop art as a form of communication; with the availability of clip art anyone can use it with the help of a photo-copier.

If people make the effort to use their imagination a little there are a number of secular videos which can be used to initiate conversations or help people to grasp Christian truths. The same is true of tape recorders, video cameras and even computers.

In the world of the Bible visual aids were always there – the sower and the seed, workers in the vineyard, the potter and the clay, the shepherd and the sheep, the lost coin. Many biblical truths were taught using visual aids.

7. Learning to tell the story in the culture

It is unlikely that you will know what the word 'scally' means unless you come from Liverpool. It's a word for a villain, somebody who's a real bad character. So in order to tell the story in the relevant culture we would tell stories of how God used scallies. For example I would talk about Jacob being a cheat, a con-man and a liar to boot, who fiddled his dad and his brother, ran off and got fiddled by his Uncle Laban who was as big a crook as him – they would understand that. It is vital to learn to talk through the Bible in the way that people understand it.

Be a *bouncer* for God. Bouncers are people that stand in doors guarding the entrance of night clubs. 'I would rather be a doorkeeper in your house,' (Psalm 84:10) takes on a whole new dimension!

Using this approach I have discovered that often God comes into the conversation in different ways. It's a starting point for discussion and sharing together, and beginning to gossip the gospel.

8. Word pictures

Some of you will know the 'Riding Lights' theatre company version of 'the Good Samaritan' known as *The Parable of the Punk Rocker*. It's a classic example of how you can put something in today's language – the vicar and the social worker went past and didn't help the guy that got mugged on the train, the punk rocker came along and helped the man who had been mugged.

Another example of the use of word pictures is something I have used with great effect on Radio Two. Take a well known theme such as westerns and relate it to the Bible. *How the West was Won* becomes the story of the book of Acts; *High Noon* tells the story of the peacemaker coming face to face with the killer – Paul's conversion; *The Good, The Bad and The Ugly* transforms the Pharisee, the Tax Collector and the Leper.

Other themes could be Musicals and the Message; *The King and I* is obvious, *My Fair Lady* can easily be Mary Magdalene, and Baloo the bear in *Jungle Book* singing 'The Bare Necessities of Life' preaches part of the Sermon on the Mount.

I come from the generation that grew up in the late fifties and early sixties and sixties music is having a revival. A lot of the younger generation are listening to it. Many of the girls who babysit round Anfield cannot afford to go out and buy CDs so they listen to the records of the parents in the houses where they babysit and so sixties music is well-known. We took sixties music and related it to the Bible.

So 'I can't get no satisfaction' and 'vanity, vanity, all is vanity' from the book of Ecclesiastes come together. People begin to unlock a passage of the Bible they had never thought of before. 'You'll never walk alone' and 'My God, my God, why have you forsaken me?' in Psalm 22 link together and folk begin to feel their way into the Word of God in a way that they would never have done in any other way.

'I did it my way' – when Saul couldn't wait for Samuel to come and offer the sacrifice and he lost his anointing as a result; 'I'd like to teach the world to sing', 'What a wonderful world',

'All you need is love', 'Stand by your man' about divorce, 'Bridge over troubled waters' ties in with nothing 'able to separate us from the love of God' in Romans 8; 'Amazing grace' and 'Those were the days' is Job reflecting on his past – and all of a sudden through the medium of music and conjuring up a word picture we are unlocking the word of God in a wonderful way into the culture. It just takes a bit of thought, time and preparation.

9. Don't give up

Don't be deterred by comings and goings and the short-term enthusiasm of people because in the long-term many come back. I will give you an example. A few years ago I was working in a church in Everton where we had a junior club with about seventy kids between the ages of about seven and eleven who would charge in and out twice a week. We decided, at the end of the club, to offer any of those who wanted the opportunity to stay on. On offer was a little bit of a 'God-slot' where we would show cartoon film strips on Bible themes, a kind of children's Bible study. Once we were showing one called *Solly Silverberg's Bonfire in Babylon* and most of these kids decided to stay behind, about sixty of them. It was a real pain; they were walking all over the chairs, making shadows in front of the projector and bashing each other. I thought, 'what a waste of time'.

What was amazing was that the following week one of them came up to me and said, 'Hey Dave! wasn't it great about that king that thought he was boss and he wasn't and them guys that got into the hot water and how God looked after them and got them out' and I thought, 'How on earth did you hear that?'

We needed to realize that a lot of these children came from households where there is noise and shouting. So all the time they were filtering out what they wanted to listen to. You and I can't make assumptions about people and say they didn't listen just because they didn't do it our way. You would be surprised how the seed of the word of God goes down deep into people's hearts just when you think nothing's happening, then much later something comes of it.

Billy was an armed bank robber, about 6 feet 3 inches tall. I remember talking to Billy because he lived just by us and often the conversation got on to things about God. Not heavy, we just talked it through lightly, and we didn't seem to be getting anywhere even though he came to a few Bible studies. Ten years later there was a knock on our door and Billy and one of his 'minders' came along to my house. He said, 'Dave, you know me, I have been a scally and I've done all sorts of things. I've hurt people. I've blown people away and stuff like that and I've tried all sorts but I haven't tried God – and I thought it was about time I gave him a go.' And this great big fellow came and knelt on his knees in our front room to ask Jesus to come into his life – ten years afterwards, when I had just given up and thought what a waste of time. That's just to encourage you not to give up.

10. Dare to be different

'Do not conform any longer to the pattern of this world' (Romans 12:2). Do you know how often we are conditioned by our own Christian upbringing and how we are sometimes frightened to experiment and find new ways of communicating the gospel?

One story that may help is about one of the preachers who was in Anfield Road Fellowship. Al used to be one of the local thugs and if you wanted to help somebody to see things your way you slipped Al a few bob, he got the lads together and he encouraged them to see things your way. He had been in and out of prison, was an alcoholic *etc*. When he was at school he was caught taking lead off the school roof and it started from there. He has been technically unemployed for over 18 years. By a long journey Al made his way into the Kingdom and joined our fellowship where he became one of our great communicators. He has never been out of Anfield, he has never learned educationally to speak at a different level. He communicates in the language of the local people.

Al came into the meeting to preach one day with a bin-liner full of rubbish. (You try not to be surprised at anything in Anfield!) He had been down the entry and found a bag of rubbish; he opened it up and proceeded to empty it in the middle of the meeting – and it stank! Then he began to talk about it; 'It's interesting what you can learn about people from their rubbish.' He commented on all the different objects of art that were coming out of this bin-liner. Then Al switched it and said, 'There's a lot of rubbish in our lives that we have got to get out and that we can't get rid of' (and, this is a theologically strange thought), 'you know, Jesus is the Good Bin-man. He will take our rubbish away but first we have got to put it out.' You could have heard a pin drop. Al had communicated in a totally different way from the rest of us and he had hit to the heart of every person who was in that situation – and they heard him, loud and clear.

There is not enough space in one chapter to share a lifetime's experiences but I hope that some of the issues I have raised will help you to think and communicate more creatively in your Bible study.

Trevor Gregory is a member of the International Co-ordinating Team for Operation Mobilisation, motivating prayer both within and outside the movement. He has previously worked with the Evangelical Alliance and Youth for Christ. Trev firmly believes that prayer is not for the selected few – we all need to learn how to pray. He is married to Denice and they live in a 19th century cottage in East Yorkshire with their three children.

Praying together

Trevor Gregory

With the Bible study drawing to a close the group senses what is coming next: the prayer time. As usual this period of time standing still is introduced with the words, 'Let's now move into a time of prayer. What matters for prayer do we have?'

Members look at each other's feet so as not to catch the attention of the leader as they search endlessly through the week's events for prayer requests. Soon the prayer shopping list is complete and the group is invited to 'lift these things to the Lord' and enter the great Prayer Supermarket of heaven. Most are apprehensive and the prayer-pause takes hold. All that can be heard is the cat snoring on the rug in the centre of the room. Soon the cat's tuneless snore is joined by other members of the group. Suddenly, the silence is shattered as the leader's wife prays about the requests, asking God to bless, heal, or encourage according to the answer required. The leader breathes a sigh of relief and suggests closing with the grace. Immediately the painful ordeal is over and the meeting springs back to life with people chattering away until going home time.

This, for many is how prayer is treated in housegroups. It's relegated to signalling the start and conclusion of the meeting. The opening prayer is usually one of thanks – thanks that people have turned up on such a wet cold winter's evening!

The Bible study may be well prepared, the fellowship may be meaningful, but the prayer life of the group is one up-hill struggle. This situation needs to be recognized and assessed before anything can be done to remedy it.

Begin this process by spending some time assessing the current prayer life of the group. How are members encouraged to pray? Are people at ease and want to pray? Are the same prayers said each week in the same way? How much preparation and thought before the meeting goes into the prayer time? How much importance is placed on prayer in the wider church fellowship; are there specific prayer meetings; how are they organized and what 'style' of prayer occurs?

For some group members prayer is a very personal act and is a set time in the worship service on Sundays when written prayers and responses are read. In such situations their prayer experience will be restricted to listening to others and silently responding. Do not condemn people who have not yet broken the prayer sound barrier. Similarly, do not expect them to be overnight expert pray-ers. Rather, in assessing the group, begin to think of ways of teaching and leading them to open times of prayer. After all, it is in the housegroup that people are more likely to have the opportunity to pray aloud and also receive teaching and coaching on prayer.

As part of your assessment of the group think through the following issues: How can you build on their prayer experience of silent prayer to praying out loud? How do members feel about the way prayer is treated in the church?

Next, list expectations for the group as far as prayer is concerned. Is the goal to reach a point where members can feel at ease to pray out loud and to try different prayer styles?

Another area leaders need to check and assess is their own prayer life. As housegroup leaders, are the expectations for the group exceeding our own experience? One danger of leadership is projecting personal spiritual failure on to the group and in so doing inverting this into high demands. When such idealized levels are not met by the group, leaders will either blame themselves or, more likely, blame the group. Throughout your assessment of yourself and the group be honest. Try to identify the issues and the current situation, and come away from this time with a good idea of your expectations for the group as well as personal prayer expectations.

Once such an assessment has been completed then a way forward can be planned. The following ideas fall into essentially two types. The first is specifically prayer orientated where the aim is to expose group members to teaching on prayer as well as to different prayer styles and models. The second section looks at how prayer can be integrated into the weekly meeting.

Prayer orientated meeting

The prayer study

One option may be to spend some time studying prayer and in particular how to pray as a group. There are quite a few courses on prayer for groups, but one particularly good one is *Saints at Prayer* by Michael Mitton which uses the Lord's Prayer in Matthew 6:9–13 as its foundation.[1] Alongside the leader's manual comes a link booklet for group members to use for further personal study.

Another helpful set of biblical prayers to study are those scattered throughout Paul's letters. By studying written prayers in the Bible we can glimpse an insight into the private spiritual life of the pray-ers and see the depth of love they had for those they prayed for as well as toward God. Through Paul's prayers we see what he has been praying for his readers and by studying such prayers we can understand more fully why his letters were written and the possible dangers being faced by the church (Colossians 1:9–12). Paul, though, not only shared what he had been praying for his readers but also encouraged them to pray for him (Colossians 4:3–4). In his excellent book, *A Call to Spiritual Reformation* D. A. Carson examines eight of Paul's prayers or requests for prayer with the purpose of learning 'what to pray for, what arguments to use, what priorities we should adopt, what beliefs should shape our prayers and much more.'[2]

Prayer outreach

This has some similarities to prayer triplets and is an adaptation of this highly successful prayer idea. In a prayer outreach the members identify non-Christian friends to pray for and embark upon ways of sharing their faith.

Before embarking on a prayer outreach discuss the scheme with the group members as a level of commitment is required. Some may feel that the housegroup is not for outreach but biblical study and Christian fellowship. Others on the other hand may find the following a helpful start into talking and sharing with their neighbours and friends. If you do embark upon a prayer outreach decide beforehand how enquirers or new Christians will be cared for afterwards.

To complete each of the four stages will take no fewer than four housegroup meetings, but encourage members to meet over and above your collective time altogether. A prayer outreach culminates in a special event which will need planning in advance.

Stage one Begin by discussing as a group how you feel about sharing your faith. Ask people to share their experiences. Bring the discussion around to uncovering the reasons why so often Christians are slow or shy in telling others about Jesus or even in engaging in spiritual conversation with non-believers. Move on in the discussion and look for solutions to the issues raised.

In this first stage each member should identify three non-Christian friends to pray for that they should become Christians. Depending on the size of the housegroup it may be helpful to suggest the group forms smaller groups of two or three. In these small groups each member introduces the three people they will be praying for. Encourage members to share a little about the people they have chosen to pray for; are they neighbours, friends, family or work colleagues? What are the issues they face that are holding them back from believing? What are the encouragements?

During the time of prayer begin by giving thanks for the non-

Christians. Encourage members to use the list of 'encouragements' to give thanks to God. After allowing sufficient time for people to pray, move on to the next prayer point.

Often we woffle in prayer and give God excuses for not answering our prayers! Therefore propose that members pray and ask that before the next housegroup each of the non-Christians named open up a spiritual conversation. As an alternative, recommend that they pray and ask for an opening for a conversation which they initiate. Whichever is suggested, ask God to allow them to listen to what people are saying as much as to share Jesus. Finally, encourage members to carry on praying throughout the coming days for their chosen three non-Christians.

Stage two At the next housegroup meeting invite members to report back on their conversations with the people they are praying for. Before discussing further the issues raised in conversation, ask three members to give thanks for answered prayer. Encourage those who have not had all of their expected conversations and pray for those members affected.

Discuss together the conversations and begin to identify the issues or barriers that are stopping these people coming to faith. Be aware that some of the conversations are confidential so do not put pressure on people to break this. Discern together whether the barriers are genuine, are red herrings, or are possibly hiding something deeper. You will find that the issues revolve around belief in God's or Jesus' existence and claim to deity; suffering; and the differences between Christianity and other world religions. Steve Chalke and Scripture Union have produced both a video and an audio cassette which consider these issues and may be of help. The 'Good Question' video or tape could be watched or listened to to help in further conversations.[3] You may wish to have copies of the video or tape available for members to give or loan to the people that they are talking to.

Invite members to form small groups of two or three, preferably with the same people as the time before. Lead a time of prayer and begin by inviting members to pray for their friends and the barriers that exist. Suggest that they ask God to meet their need and begin to dismantle the barriers. After people have prayed in their groups for this, invite members to pray for each other and for a further opportunity to talk with their non-Christian friends. During this time of prayer, pray for those non-Christians who are being prayed for but have not opened up to a spiritual conversation and ask God again for an opportunity to share with them.

Stage three This involves reviewing the week's progress but also planning for stage four, the open meeting. As with stage two, have a brief time of testimony concerning the conversations held then stop and give thanks for what God is doing and for answered prayer.

Discuss in detail the conversations and ascertain if there has been any movement or developments in the non-Christians. Once again see what collective wisdom and help the group can give to one another. Using the information gained out of the conversations, pray together for the non-Christians and ask for an opportunity to invite them to an open housegroup or event.

Stage four Spend time discussing the way forward and look at the possibility of holding an open meeting for non-Christian friends to attend. Decide together if this meeting will be a friendly low-key evangelistic meeting where they are invited to attend an enquirers' course like 'Alpha'[4] or 'Just Looking'[5]. Or will the evening together have a clear presentation of the gospel? Whichever format stage four takes, pray as a group for God's blessing on the venture and ask specifically once again that people will become Christians.

Passover

Often we consider prayer only in terms of asking either for ourselves or on behalf of others. Yet there is much more to prayer than that, and we need to rediscover the richness, diversity and depth that can be experienced in developing a prayer life both as a group and as individuals. The use of liturgical prayer, symbolism and meaning can lead people into a new response in prayer, worship and adoration toward God. One of the best ways I've found of achieving this is by holding a passover meal.

Throughout the Old Testament the people of Israel are told to observe the Passover 'as a lasting ordinance for you and your descendants' (Exodus 12:24). Their exodus and redemption from Egypt was a proof that God had chosen them to be his people and that he was their God, 'I will take you as my own people, and I will be your God. Then you will know that I am the LORD, your God, who brought you out from under the yoke of the Egyptians' (Exodus 6:7). This unique relationship was to show God's direct and personal involvement in the lives of the people. Centuries later, at the same time of year as Israel celebrated their physical freedom from slavery, God acted again by providing spiritual freedom. Jesus became the redeemer, sacrificed on the cross to free mankind from the slavery of sin.

If you want to pursue the idea of celebrating a Passover with your group, the author will be happy to oblige you with an abbreviated and adapted form of the service. Write to him c/o Crossway Books, 38 De Montfort Street, Leicester, LE1 7GP, UK. For a detailed discussion of the subject see Martha Zimmerman's *Celebrate the Feasts*[6].

Around the world

Many find praying for foreign countries and situations difficult, often through lack of understanding of what it's like to live in a different culture, speak a different language, and eat different food. The 'out of sight, out of mind' mentality often can be applied to many Christians when it comes to praying for missionaries. However, with a little creative thinking a specialized housegroup dedicated to prayer for such places can be achieved easily.

Each country focus evening can include food, music, information-sharing, and prayer. First choose the country you are wanting to pray for. Then visit the cookery section of your local library and find out what is eaten. Food is a great way of enabling people to begin to 'experience' and put themselves in the shoes of believers in foreign countries.

Music can also convey an atmosphere, so while you're in the library visit the music section and talk to the librarian about the country concerned and its music. Use the music in the background throughout the evening.

Next refer to Operation World[7], the guide to praying for the world. Under each nation there are prayer points and information concerning the particular country's spiritual, political and economic state. Use the economic and political information to devise a quiz for members to complete as they arrive. Compile the spiritual information and after eating and discussing the nation and its customs, share the information. Operation World mentions various agencies that are working in each nation; write to one or two of these asking for further information or for a contact number and arrange to phone a missionary in that particular nation and ask about prayer needs. Alternatively if the church already has contacts in the selected country, arrange to phone or fax them during the evening.

Now that people are beginning to understand and possibly appreciate the situation in the chosen nation, it is time to pray. Prayer information can be based on Operation World, the missionary, and agency. Use one or more of the prayer activities detailed later in the chapter. The housegroup I attend had a Hong Kong evening and the leaders had taken the 'fortune' out of each Fortune Cookie and replaced them with a prayer request.

Integrating prayer

Holding dedicated prayer housegroups or studying prayer is only part of the picture. Such meetings may be well thought of but the following week, in the normal housegroup meeting, the prayer time can be deadly again; after all, old habits die hard!

When preparing a housegroup meeting be thinking also

about the prayer element. What are you going to encourage people to pray about and how are you going to ask people to pray? The what and the how of prayer are crucial if the prayer element is going to be more than a group of people sitting in the shampoo position, gently massaging their dandruff into the carpet.

Often the easy part is finding and supplying information of what we want people to pray about. Christian books like Operation World, organizations' magazines, even the church's newsletter and weekly news sheet, can supply plenty of information for prayer. The leader needs to decide not only if it is relevant to the theme of the meeting, but also how the information is communicated and used in order that a constructive prayer time can be held.

The use of simple prayer frameworks can be easily devised to integrate the prayer time into the main theme of the evening. If the group activity is a Bible study, then devise a prayer frame-work by using the main points from the passage or truths being discussed. Let's use for example, a study of Ephesians 2:19–22, and refer to Stephen Motyer's commentary in the *Crossway Bible Guide*[8]. The main discussion points centre around the three pictures Paul uses to describe the Ephesians now they are in Christ; 'fellow-citizens' (verse 19), 'members of God's house hold' (verse 19), and 'a holy temple in the Lord' (verse 21). These discussion points can be used as a prayer framework by focusing firstly on thanks that we are citizens through Jesus' death and resurrection; secondly, by focusing on the needs of the church and other members of the church 'household'. The third stem of the framework centres on being a holy temple. Here the focus is on group members and their desire to be holy and in unity with the rest of the church household.

Once it has been decided what to pray for, the next stage is to decide how to pray. What are we going to ask people to 'do' as they pray – sit, stand, kneel, write their prayer, or something far more creative. There is more to prayer than sitting with clasped hands and eyes tight shut. In fact the Bible does not mention that closing eyes is the way to pray; Jesus looked toward heaven in John 17:1, while Paul suggests lifting holy hands up to God. Therefore, it is important that 'how to' pray is addressed just as much as 'what to' pray for.

Below are a number of ideas and prayer activities to use in housegroups. Each needs to be fitted into a prayer framework. The list is not exhaustive but I hope it is sufficient to help stimulate your own ideas and creativity. Some of the activities suggest that the group is split into smaller groups; quite often this helps the quieter members to pray as it is less intimidating. However, sometimes the housegroup size is small so it may be inappropriate to split the group.

Bible prayer

This is a good way of praying the Psalms, but can be used for other passages too. Split the group into groups of three and number each member 1, 2 and 3. Number 1 reads the first verse and then using some of the thoughts and imagery prays a short prayer. Number 2 then reads verse 2 and prays in the same way. Number 3 does the same and then the process is repeated with number 1 reading the fourth verse and praying. Continue in this way until the passage is complete.

Gifts

When studying and discussing the gifts of the Holy Spirit the following prayer activity helps to focus on not only the gift but also the giver. Have a selection of gift-wrapped boxes each labelled inside with one of the gifts of the Spirit from the lists found in 1 Corinthians 12, Ephesians 4, or Romans 12. Distribute the boxes around the group and after the gifts have been opened suggest people pray for that particular gift to be released in the church and housegroup more powerfully. This could be done in pairs if you have more members than gift boxes.

Fruit salad

According to the owner of the vegetable shop I used to work in, Granny Smith – who is famous for the distinguished apple of the same name – used to say, 'Life is one rich fruit salad!' Based on the advice and instructions of the apostle Paul in Galatians 5:22–23, we should be desiring the rich salad of the fruit of the Spirit.

Have nine different types of fruit available. Cut each into portions and place them in a bowl labelled with the name of one of the fruits of the Spirit. Invite group members to select three fruits of the Spirit that they would like to grow and develop in their lives or in the life of their family. They then take the corresponding piece of fruit to the fruit of the Spirit they have chosen. For example, if apples represent the fruit of the Spirit 'love' and someone wants to see love develop in themselves or family, then they take a portion of apple.

There are now two ways to proceed with this prayer activity; either allow members to pray silently for themselves and the particular situation they are thinking of which requires this fruit of the Spirit. Or alternatively suggest that members share with their neighbour why they chose that particular fruit of the Spirit and then they pray for each other.

News – words and pictures

Often it is difficult to pray for the starving millions or the thousands of homeless affected by civil war. Some members of the group may sense the need for prayer for such situations, but also are paralysed by the enormity of the problem. Pictures from either newspapers or video recorded from the TV newscasts are a great prayer resource. If people are finding the situation hard to understand the 'why it's happening' and want to pray for the people, then encourage them to pray for the people they see in the pictures.

To use newspapers in the meeting find stories out of local/and or national papers for the group to pray for. Distribute these around the group and ask people to pray for these situations. Draw members' attention to the pictures and headlines, for often these help to crystallize what to pray for.

When using video news clips it is often helpful to show the news item with the commentary. Then rewind the tape and play it again this time with the sound turned down as people either pray silently or aloud. Suggest they pray with their eyes open watching the screen. On the last picture pause the video and allow prayer to continue.

Written prayers

There are some people who are very uncomfortable with praying aloud. Often encouraging them to write their prayers helps. This can either be done by suggesting they write them before the meeting or by having a time of prayer when everyone present writes a prayer.

Prayer-walking

Some churches are beginning to look at the prayer life of their fellowship and are encouraging housegroups to 'prayer-walk' the neighbourhood where they meet. Prayer-walking is one way of visibly reminding the Christians of the needs in their area and of the churches calling to be salt and light.

There are various ways of prayer-walking. One method is to suggest to members that as they walk in twos or threes they pray together for families and the homes of people they pass. Remember the old, lonely, unemployed, those with disabilities, children and young people. Another time the group could prayer-walk the neighbourhood and stop and pray for the community institutions; the churches, police station, schools, doctors' surgery, law courts, youth club, *etc*. Alternatively, the venture could be a progressive prayer-walk where the group walk from one church member's home to the next praying for the witness of the church in the neighbourhood and praying a blessing on the homes and households of the church members visited.

Snowball

Sometimes the prayer time suddenly comes to an abrupt end when all the issues have been prayed for once. Often some members want to pray about the same issue but because someone has beaten them to it they sit there silent having missed their chance. In 'Snowball', the group is encouraged to agree with the previous prayer; expand on it; and deepen it.

Some of these suggestions may help you, others may not. Choose those that are most appropriate for your group. Perhaps these ideas will stimulate you to explore others. Try to strike the balance between getting stuck in an over-familiar rut and confusing everyone with too much innovation; and may your prayers be answered!

Notes

1 Michael Mitton, *Saints at Prayer* (Linx Communications /Anglican Renewal Ministries, 1994).
2 D. A. Carson, *A Call to Spiritual Reformation* (Inter-Varsity Press, 1992). Each chapter has a set of questions at the end that could easily be adapted for group use. An excellent resource for an established group.
3 Steve Chalke, *Good Question – the Video* (Scripture Union, 1994). Steve Chalke, *Good Question – the Tape* (Scripture Union, 1993).
4 For further information and details on the Alpha Course see: Nicky Gumble, *Telling Others: The Alpha Initiative* (Kingsway, 1994).
5 For further information and details on the Just Looking materials see: John Allan, *Just Looking* (The Bible Society, 1995).
6 Martha Zimmerman, *Celebrate the Feasts of the Old Testament in Your Home or Church* (Bethany House Publishers, USA, 1981), pp. 49–93.
7 Patrick Johnson, *Operation World* (OM Publishing, 5th edition, 1993).
8 Stephen Motyer, *Ephesians – Free to be One* (*Crossway Bible Guides*, Crossway Books, 1994, pp. 75–77.

Peter Meadows tends to get involved with starting things, including Spring Harvest, Tear Fund and Premier – London's Christian radio station.

Rosemary, his wife, combines running her small catering company with being a doctor's receptionist. Like several of her children, she also works as a TV and film extra.

Both enjoy eating out and foreign travel. Rosemary having cancer at thirty – followed by several years of depressive illness – taught them much about the need for honesty and togetherness in the church.

Their best ever housegroup was when they were 'between churches' and everyone needed to cling on to each other for survival. They nicknamed it 'the lifeboat.'

Peter and Rosemary have lived in Chessington, Surrey for some twenty-six years, gathering five children, aged 24 to 13, on the way.

Sharing

Peter and Rosemary Meadows

The first Christians had a word for togetherness: *koinonia*. It described people putting their love for God into action by being genuinely caring, concerned and supportive of each other.

Your housegroup is the key to creating such an experience of togetherness, where people belong to one another, are accepted, valued and loved. Where openness, honesty, practical care and healing, in its fullest sense, are the order of the day. What we are talking about is the authentic expression of what it really means to be Christians. If only this were the automatic result of putting a dozen or so enthusiastic and committed Christians in a room together for a couple of hours each week. But such a goal can only be reached through commitment and practical action.

So let's look at some practical steps that a housegroup can take in order to move from simply meeting together to where they are meeting each other's needs.

Be clear of your goal

Bible knowledge that does no more than equip us to play a game of Bible Trivial Pursuits is of no ultimate value, no matter how good it may make anyone feel. The challenge is to put the Bible to work so that it turns what people learn into life-enhancing activity. To settle for anything less than the authentic Christian experience described above will be selling everyone short.

Your goal is to help create an environment where people are mutually open, honest, vulnerable, supportive and caring. This is to include everyone, even those who, at present, sit shyly in the corner and seem to apply superglue to their lips en route to the meeting.

For too long, individual and personal piety has been the goal of Christian teaching. However, the command and example of Scripture is that we are to be 'one-another' people. Your housegroup is the arena to make this happen. After all, what other environment is there in which to fulfil the following commands.

- 'Be devoted to one another' (Romans 12:10a)
- 'Honour one another' (Romans 12:10b)
- 'Live in harmony with one another' (Romans 12:16)
- 'Accept one another' (Romans 15:7)
- Express 'equal concern for each other' (1 Corinthians 12:25)
- 'Serve one another in love' (Galatians 5:13)
- 'Carry each other's burdens' (Galatians 6:2)
- 'Be kind and compassionate to one another, forgiving each other' (Ephesians 4:32)
- 'Speak to one another with psalms, hymns and spiritual songs' (Ephesians 5:19)
- 'Submit to one another' (Ephesians 5:21)
- 'Look . . . to the interests of others' (Philippians 2:4)
- 'Bear with each other' (Colossians 3:13a)
- 'Forgive whatever grievances you may have against one another' (Colossians 3:13b)
- 'Counsel one another' (Colossians 3:16)
- 'May the Lord make your love increase and overflow for each other' (1 Thessalonians 3:12)
- 'Encourage each other' (1 Thessalonians 4:18)
- 'Encourage one another daily' (Hebrews 3:13)
- 'Spur one another on towards love and good deeds' (Hebrews 10:24)
- 'Encourage one another' (Hebrews 10:25)

- 'Do not slander one another' (James 4:11)
- 'Confess your sins to each other' (James 5:16a)
- 'Pray for each other' (James 5:16b)
- 'Love each other deeply' (1 Peter 4:8)
- 'Offer hospitality to one another without grumbling' (1 Peter 4:9)
- 'Clothe yourselves with humility towards one another' (1 Peter 5:5)
- 'Love one another' (1 John 3:11)

Don't rush

A group made up of mere acquaintances will not become intimate friends overnight – no matter how much encouragement they are given to make the transition. We have witnessed throats go dry, hearts pump and faces turn white when some enthusiast launched into 'deep-end' questions like, 'So where are you struggling in your Christian life right now?'

Of course, there are a few extrovert, self-confident individuals who are just waiting for the opportunity to let it all hang out. But most people need an environment of mutual trust and acceptance before they are ready to peep out from behind their mask. The process of creating open and honest relationships cannot accelerate from a standing start to 70mph in three seconds without a severe crunching of gears.

Understand why togetherness does not happen spontaneously

Some people hold back from building deep relationships – and from being willing to disclose their personal needs and concerns – because they are shy and reserved by nature. But there are a multitude of other reasons.

We think of Brian, who was clearly intimidated into silence because he felt that everyone else knew so much more than he did; of June who seemed afraid of showing herself up by saying something foolish or inappropriate. The fear of being laughed at, or seen to be immature or less than competent was enough to sideline her in the group.

Audrey was aware of the way private disclosures could so swiftly and easily become public gossip and that was too great a risk for her to take. This should remind us that any personal and private sharing *must* be kept in the strictest confidence within the group. If there are any 'leaks', trust is shattered.

There are thousands of such 'Brians', 'Junes' and 'Audreys'. They create a major roadblock on the journey towards togetherness, but it can be dismantled.

Look for ways to help people open up

The journey towards togetherness involves people moving from being strangers to being friends. Such a journey takes more than a room, some coffee and some Bibles. An essential ingredient is to recognize the humanity of those involved. Indeed, many housegroups get stuck because they are so spiritually focused that those involved have to leave their 'normalness' at the door as they enter.

One evening with a housegroup we asked people to scan the pages of the gospels in order to create two lists. The first was of those things that Jesus did that were spiritual or supernatural. The other was a list of the ordinary and human things Jesus did. When the exercise was over, it made a tremendous impact to see how much longer the second list was and what it included.

As a result, we captured a picture of Jesus who sailed a boat, cooked breakfast for his friends, sang a hymn, rode a donkey, ate with friends, and so on. This emphasizes the normality of the relationship between Jesus and his followers, and his followers and each other. An essential element in creating togetherness is to explore that dimension of humanness. A key step in the process is for people to share with the group those things that go to make them the person they are: from the past, present and future.

The *past* includes the events, people, places and environment that have helped to shape who they are today. For example, Ruth's loss of her sister, Dave's redundancy, Ena's childhood in a mill town, the example of Jack's athletics coach all reveal something and all help to make connections with the rest of the group.

The same is true of the *present*. No mutual spiritual journey is really possible without understanding each other's values, interests, problems and difficulties. While the *future* – what they are aiming for – is made up of those things that they are working towards, and hoping and praying for.

Togetherness does not spring from meetings that are exclusively 'to study the word', followed by some prayer requests. Togetherness grows as people gain confidence in sharing the 'whos, whats and wheres' of their life, as this helps others to understand and empathize with them. As a result, the group see themselves as having lives entwined with each other's. Respect and understanding grow.

This emphasis on people speaking of who they are, and where they are going, has the added advantage that no-one need be left out. Contributions do not depend on having sound Bible knowledge; there are no right or wrong answers that bring the risk of someone looking foolish.

Few people naturally open up in detail as to how they became who they are. But there are some tried and tested ways to help them. The following examples can be used either as they are or adapted to suit your needs.

The shield

Give each person in the group a large piece of paper and a felt-tip pen. Ask them to draw a simple shield divided into four quarters. Explain that this is to become their personal coat of arms.

In each of the four quarters they are to draw something representing a different aspect of their life, past or present. Show them your own coat of arms as an example. Make sure your drawings are very simple and unprofessional, to avoid anyone feeling threatened.

When the shields are completed, each person briefly explains what they have drawn and why.

The truth game

One of the group, after being given a little while to think, owns up to:

- Their earliest memory
- Their favourite music as a teenager
- The way they most like to spend their spare time now.

However, one of their answers must be a lie and the rest of the group are to guess which.

This can be played in groups of up to six people, where the group try to reach a common agreement as to the right answer. In a larger group, people could indicate their individual answer by a show of hands. In which case there should be a prize for the one who gets the most right answers. In a small group everyone can have a turn to lie. In a larger group, just select a few people.

Saved from the fire

Give each group member a piece of paper with the same list of objects on it such as:

- Your most treasured item of clothing
- An album with all your photographs of the past five years
- An almost finished poem that you have been working on for a year
- An irreplaceable book borrowed from a friend
- Your appointments diary
- Letters from your first true love
- The brooch/watch handed down from your great-grandmother/father
- The model aeroplane you created aged eleven when ill in bed for six weeks
- Your collection of rare stamps worth £10,000
- Your goldfish.

Each group member is to assume that their house is on fire, and there is only time to grab three of the items on the list. Which would they choose? Give them a few minutes to decide. Then ask them, in turn, to share their list with the rest of the group.

Time lines

Ask people to draw a long horizontal line on a piece of paper. Explain that this line represents their life from birth until now. They are to put two vertical lines onto the horizontal line so as to divide it into three roughly equal parts, presenting three periods of their life.

A time line like this can be used to help people reveal aspects of their life in a variety of non-threatening ways. For example:

- Ask them to write in each section the name of one person who they most admired – or who most influenced them.
- Ask them to draw weather symbols or road signs at relevant places along the line to represent how they saw themselves relating to God at those points in their life.
- Ask them to draw the actual line in a way that indicates how they remember their relationship to God at the time.

In each case, show the group your own example in order to make sure people understand, and to set an example of openness and honesty.

Honesty

Use the questions that follow, adapted and expanded as you wish, as the basis for an honesty session. This is a particularly good way to launch any new housegroup.

The questions could each be written on separate pieces of paper which are folded and put in a box or bag. Group members take it in turns to take one and to answer the question that it poses. They return the question to the box which can go round the group several times. Anyone picking a question that they have already answered puts it back and takes another. Or the questions could be written up as spokes of a wheel with a spinner fixed in the centre. People take it in turns to spin to see which question they should answer. Or, number the questions from one to twenty, and get people to throw a dart in a dart board to select their question.

- My longest journey as a teenager
- My first kiss outside of my family
- How my home was heated as a child
- The first record that I ever bought
- Who I would call first to share some great news
- The person who encouraged me most as a child
- My favourite childhood story
- The relation, other than my parents, whose home I loved to visit
- The teacher I liked best and why
- My childhood fear or phobia
- The subjects I enjoyed most and least at school
- What I wore to my first dance
- The first real recipe I cooked
- The childhood or teenage friend I most wish I could meet again
- My first-ever job and how much I earned for it
- The Christian who influenced me considerably
- The time my parents found me out
- My favourite fantasy character as a child
- The time I was really scared
- The person I most wanted to be like as a teenager
- The item that has no real value that I treasure most
- My dream holiday.

Bible identification

When working with the Bible in the housegroup, look for ways in which people can identify themselves with the characters and incidents being covered. For example, coming to the end of a series on the gospels, we asked the housegroup to each identify which of the people who met Jesus they felt was most like them. Mary took a long time before saying, 'The woman who touched Jesus in the crowd. She was desperate and knew the only hope was to reach out to him. I need to do the same.' And she did.

Examples to help you think through this approach include:

The fruit of the Spirit Ask people to identify one of the fruits that they see present in the life of someone in the group.
The wedding of Cana Which of the people in the story do they feel is most like them and why.
The feeding of the five thousand Which role do they think they would have played if they had been there at the time.
The Beatitudes Identify the Beatitude that the group most see present in the life of another group member. Do this for all the group.

(The best source for group material that explores this approach is Small Group Resources, 1 Hilton Place, Harehills, Leeds LS8 4HE.)

Tell them it's OK

The journey towards togetherness will grind to a halt unless people enjoy the encouragement and affirmation they need to spur them on. In each of the above activities it is essential to find ways for people to receive feedback that tells them their contribution has been valued. For example, in the shield exercise, ask group members to each say one thing they liked about someone else's contribution. In many of the other activities, you can ask people to comment on one thing that someone has said that helped or encouraged them.

A practical exercise to affirm other members of the group is to ask each person to take a piece of paper, and to write their name on it. Pass each piece of paper two places to the left. The person who receives it adds to the paper a word or phrase that expresses something for which they value the person named (honesty, reliability, faithfulness, cheerfulness, *etc.*). The paper is passed on another two places. Now the group members each pray a *brief* prayer for the person named on the paper they hold, giving thanks for what they are valued for.

An essential part of affirmation is to squash any judgmental attitudes. People are not there to tell each other how to live, but to make a journey together. Athletics coaches know that if they are to keep people motivated each negative comment must be set in the context of at least eight positive ones. The people in your housegroup are no different.

Encourage open personal objectives

Most people have private hopes, dreams and goals on their spiritual agenda. These take on a new dimension when the rest of the group know and are in prayerful support.

Such openness only comes when the group are some way on the road to togetherness. It involves people feeling safe enough to identify openly the areas of their life where they feel they need God's help, or other people's – or both. They will feel safe only if they know that their openness will not be repeated outside the group. This point is worth emphasizing. Such openness though means facing questions such as:

- In six months I would like to look back and see that I have become . . .
- At the moment my area of spiritual struggle is . . .
- It seems to me that what God is wanting from me is . . .
- The hurt in my life that I most need God's help with now is . . .

Such questions are a practical way to apply the implications of a passage of scripture that has been studied.

Do things together

There are those, particularly of an older generation, who keep the sacred and secular in quite separate departments of their life. To them, praying together and playing together are at totally different ends of the scale in terms of the measure of approval that God has for them. It is essential that you, as the leader of the group – and the group as a whole – do not fall into the same trap, even subconsciously.

We express our God-given humanity when we are enjoying the company of others and enriching them with our presence – whether praying or playing. We do not meet together in normal relationships 'in order' to achieve some goal, but because God created us to enjoy the richness of relationships. This means that those 'non-spiritual' activities that your group does are not added extras, but an essential and equal part of the journey towards togetherness.

Many a group has discovered that relationships build more quickly and deeply when sharing a task like church cleaning. The lesson here is to look for ways to run projects together. Practically, this may need the involvement of one or more other housegroups. The possibilities are endless:

- A fund-raising car wash in the church car park
- A monster garage sale
- A swimming gala
- A Valentines dance
- A garden party and barbecue.

Social events can be equally helpful. We still have great memories of the evening that twenty or so of us spent having a party that mainly involved playing games usually reserved for nine-year-olds. One game involved two teams either side of a row of chairs that served as a net. Each team was given a stack of old newspapers, which they rolled into balls. At a given signal, they had five minutes to get as much paper onto their opponents' side of the net as possible. What mess! What mayhem! What fun!

Eat together

Study the eating habits of Jesus and you will swiftly recognize the significance of sharing food together. However, when following this example, as you must, remember that togetherness is threatened by anything that generates a sense of competitive spirit, envy or pride. So keep the food simple to prevent people trying to outdo each other or feeling they have to keep up.

The most straightforward approach is to ask everyone to bring something. Designate the task of 'main dish', 'salad', 'dessert' and so on among the group, and take what comes. Easy ideas for food include all kinds of pasta, baked potatoes, salads and dips. Try a fondue night. Or you could make it a themed evening. For example, an Hawaiian night, with fancy dress, lots of pineapple and some suitable background music. The task of putting on such an evening can be as helpful in creation of togetherness as the event itself.

For events that need a simple non-alcoholic fruit punch try:

Punch for forty people

Make 4 pints of tea using sixteen tea bags. Add 2lbs of white sugar. Allow to go cold and add eight cartons of tropical fruit juice. Just before serving, add one bottle of lemonade and slices of apple, orange and lemon.

Don't be too literal over the above quantities. If the punch is running out, just add more fruit juice and lemonade.

Recognize the greatest barrier

The level of togetherness that your group reaches will be limited by the group leader's willingness to be honest and vulnerable. No-one will take their mask off while yours is still firmly in place. But pace yourself by setting examples that are within people's reach to emulate. Don't set examples that are beyond their reach and are, therefore, intimidating.

Progress also depends on your ability to demonstrate acceptance and empathy when people begin to be real. Showing that you understand how people feel will make a very positive contribution. Consider the impact on the individuals and the rest of the group when you say something like: 'David, that must have hurt you a lot'; 'Helen, I can imagine you finding that very frustrating'; 'Mike, it must have taken a lot of courage to tell us all that.'

It also means owning and accepting your emotions. The New Testament speaks of weeping with those who weep. Tears and emotional distress are all part of a normal Christian life. We are to own up to our own pain. And to stand with others in theirs – listening, caring and not judging.

Recognize that, ultimately, only God can do it

Genuine togetherness is an expression of love for one another. This is not something that can be worked up, manipulated or organized. The kind of sacrificial love needed to break down barriers and to cause people to accept and serve others can only come from God himself. It is the fruit of his Holy Spirit.

This means that all your efforts to create togetherness will have only superficial results unless there is a genuine overflow of love created by the Holy Spirit in the lives of the group. However, such a work of the Holy Spirit, by itself, may not be enough to generate practical and continuing togetherness. Indeed, all your thoughtful action can provide the arena in which the work of the Holy Spirit can be seen and demonstrated in the lives of others.

Ian Parkinson is vicar of Emmanuel Church, Saltburn, a small town on the north-east coast. He is one of a team of twelve advisers in Evangelism for the Diocese of York and, as well as helping other churches to grow in effectiveness in evangelism, regularly leads university missions.

Ian is married to Nadine and they have three children under ten years of age. Not surprisingly, for one who has very rarely ventured outside the borders of Yorkshire, Ian is passionate about cricket and still plays regularly for the local club and the Church of England clergy XI. When not playing or watching sport he may be found listening to or playing New Orleans jazz or painting in watercolours.

Bridgebuilding: using a housegroup for evangelism

Ian Parkinson

Roy was a long-distance lorry driver whose wife, Sue, had recently come to faith. Despite being intrigued at the change he saw taking place in Sue, Roy resolutely refused her repeated invitations to come to church with her. In his own mind, he just wasn't *that* type of person.

However, an invitation to a buffet supper in a house in a neighbouring street seemed a far more attractive proposition, even though he had been informed that, later on in the evening, somebody (me!) would be saying a bit about what Jesus has to offer people today. The names of some of the other people who would be there were already familiar; Sue had often mentioned them in conversation when she talked about the housegroup meetings she now attended and so obviously enjoyed.

So Roy came, looking a tiny bit awkward, had a drink, some food, got into conversation with one or two others, shared a joke or two and visibly relaxed. He listened carefully to the short talk and to the questions that followed. Time flew by. It had been a great evening. Perhaps he ought to find out more . . . He was in church the following Sunday.

Mike was newly married and a little unsettled. Around the time of his wedding he had made contact again with an old schoolfriend whom he had not seen for two or three years. In that time, the friend had been away at college and was now a committed Christian. The difference in him was staggering to Mike. What was particularly unsettling was that the friend seemed to have found something for which Mike himself was desperately searching. But Mike had been a church choirboy in earlier years. Church was something he had left behind when he had grown up. And anyway, how could something so numbingly boring have anything to say to him today.

When the invitation came to attend an event organized by the friend's housegroup, Mike leaped at it. He couldn't wait to hear the speaker begin his advertised short talk on the significance of Jesus Christ for today. Through the evening, things began to fall into place. Two months later Mike became a Christian.

I first met Jane, now a member of our church, at a dinner party, arranged by members of a housegroup, at which I had been asked to speak. She was desperately hungry spiritually, a little confused by her background and past experience, and full of questions. The evening gave her the opportunity to talk through her questions, air her fears and find a way through some of her confusion. She readily agreed to join a 'Just Looking' course and, several months later, committed her life to Christ.

These three stories of people with whom I have been involved over the years, and many others, are striking illustrations of the vital role small groups can play in the work of evangelism. Indeed, for the ten years in which I have been actively involved in leading missions in churches, universities and colleges, I have always seen this type of small-group gathering as the backbone of the mission, and as clearly the most effective method of helping others hear and evaluate the gospel of Jesus Christ.

The advantages of the small group

It's not too difficult to pick out several clear strengths of small-group evangelism just from the stories told above.

1. Many people feel uncomfortable at the prospect of entering a church building. No matter how good the preaching at our

guest services, no matter how uplifting the worship and snappy the drama group, effective evangelism doesn't take place because the threshold of the church door is just too forbidding for many to cross it. We find it frustratingly difficult to get friends and family to the place where they might hear the gospel explained.

The reasons for this are many and varied. Some have had bad or disappointing experiences of 'church' in the past, and their expectations of what might meet them if they attended a service does not fill them with excitement. Others feel uncomfortable in an environment where they don't know anyone else. They have the impression of being 'outsiders' and are terrified at the prospect of showing their ignorance of hymns, the order of service, when and where to sit and stand and so on. Even could they be cajoled into a service they would be so on edge that little might percolate through. Some people simply feel guilty because they haven't set foot in a church for years and are afraid that the minister (and other worshippers) will look down on them.

Most people, however, are quite happy visiting other people's homes. Faithful evangelism will always attempt to remove as many social and cultural barriers as possible to people hearing the gospel. Presenting the gospel at gatherings on familiar (to them!) territory is part of this process.

2. Many people have big spiritual questions but no forum in which to air them or in which to chew them over. An essential part of the small-group gathering is open discussion following the main presentation. For Jane it was this focused discussion which helped her, for the first time, to face up to some of the issues which were 'sticking points' for her in terms of coming to faith in Christ.

Other people feel quite unclear about their own spiritual understanding. They cannot articulate their own difficulties about the Christian faith. Listening in on discussion and hearing others express their own feelings is often useful in helping the unsure or confused to find a way through the fog which sometimes seems to cloud their thinking.

3. One of the 'buzz phrases' of recent years has been 'The medium is the message'; which, in everyday terms, means that we say as much by the manner in which we communicate as we do through the actual words that we speak. Our 'style' of evangelism is vitally important, especially as all surveys suggest that most unconverted people have fewer problems with the gospel of Jesus Christ than they do with the Christians who proclaim it! Housegroup evangelism treats agnostics and their opinions with respect. People are listened to, not just 'preached at'. Furthermore, we hope, in inviting guests to one of these gatherings, to commend the Lord whom we serve as we offer them a sincere and hospitable welcome, and that the glimpse they get into the life of the church will help to allay any fears or reservations they may previously have had, and which may have kept them from hearing the gospel.
4. Evangelism may be seen as a process involving three broad phases: making contact with someone, explaining the Christian good news, inviting a response. People need to hear and understand the gospel before they can be expected to respond to its challenge. In my experience, small-group evangelism works best when its role is seen as one of explaining the gospel, though of course, any faithful explanation will include a mention of the response which Jesus Christ demands to his offer. The fact that people are rarely converted outright at these kind of meetings should not, therefore, discourage us. The most difficult thing in evangelism is not usually inviting a response from those who have heard, but rather finding ways of introducing the message to those who have never heard. Small groups represent a wonderful way of doing this.

Using housegroups for evangelism

Existing church housegroups are ideal agencies for this form of evangelism for a number of reasons.
1. Small-group evangelism aims to reach families and friends of group members. An essential part of the activities of any

housegroup will be to share the evangelistic concerns of its members, to pray for unconverted friends and family members, and to offer mutual support and encouragement in personal witness. Evangelistic events arise very naturally out of such concern.

2. Housegroups often meet on a geographical basis. Not only can they pray meaningfully and effectively for their local area, but there is a much greater chance that our friends may already be acquainted with other members of our housegroup and may feel more confident of going to their homes or to an event where they already know many of those who will be present.

3. Many housegroups are able to organize a regular programme of social events, a key purpose of which is to draw in those who are not yet Christians. One such group in our last church laid on a brilliant array of walks, quiz evenings, tenpin bowling and fish and chip suppers at regular intervals. When, during the course of a church mission, they organized an outreach evening, there was no shortage of non-Christians who were more than happy to come and who felt quite at home.

4. Having a clear evangelistic dimension is vital to the health of any housegroup. It keeps a group sharp, and prevents complacency. One of the tasks of each housegroup in our own church is to organize at least one faith-sharing event each year. This emphasis gives a certain focus to the whole life of the group.

Organizing the event

How, then, might we go about organizing an evangelistic event as a housegroup? What form should the event take, and what plans and preparations need to be made?

Prayerful planning is clearly of the essence. Ask each member of the group prayerfully to consider their friends and other contacts, asking God for wisdom as to whom they might invite. Some of our friends are clearly hungry spiritually and it is certainly best to begin with such people. Encourage people to let God impress upon their hearts other friends and acquaintances whom God wants them to invite. At the next group meeting, each one will be prayed for by name.

It may be that the list of contacts is far too long for all to be accommodated at one single meeting. The ideal size for such a gathering is ten to eighteen, with non-Christians outnumbering Christians by at least three to two. There is no harm in holding two or more events if necessary, and even being able to offer friends a choice of dates. The size of rooms in group members' homes is the great determining factor in numbers of people attending. You need to choose a venue where sufficient people can be accommodated without too much of a squash, and where advance preparation on the day of the event can take place without hindrance. Often a household which has young children is not the best venue as hosts will be preoccupied with putting offspring to bed at the time when they need to be free to welcome guests and oversee final preparations.

Having established our list of contacts it is time to devise the most suitable event for those who will be there. Events where food is served always seem to work best. Buffet suppers, pudding parties, Indian food evenings are all possibilities. In certain areas a full-blown dinner party would be the normal way of socializing and therefore this would be the obvious format for an evangelistic small-group event. Use your imagination and your knowledge of what would best suit your 'target-group' as you plan your event. Buffet suppers are the most common in my experience. The housegroup members all provide food and drink, making sure that the menu is appetising and plentiful. One of the housegroup members is detailed to look after the planning of this side of the evening and to make sure that not everyone brings rice salad!

The talk or presentation similarly, needs to 'scratch where people are itching', and take as its starting point some area of reasonably common concern to our guests. 'What's gone wrong with the world?'; 'Is anybody there?'; 'Who cares?'; 'Why does God allow suffering?', are all possible themes for the evening. If a sizeable number of those invited have experienced bereavement we may choose to tackle an issue such as 'Loneliness', or

'The defeat of death' or something similar. In many gatherings, to get someone simply to tell their own story of faith is often the most effective thing of all, especially if it is someone who is from a similar background or of similar experience to many of the guests.

A suitable speaker needs to be invited and briefed. Your choice of speaker will be affected by the guests you are hoping will be there. It is vital that she or he is able to communicate effectively with them and is at home in a discussion setting. A minister or vicar is not always the most suitable choice for a speaker. Some ministers are far too accustomed to being in preaching-mode to be of any great use in a discussion evening.

Furthermore, many people clam up when in the presence of the clergy and are far more reluctant to share their own thoughts and opinions.

Well in advance of the event friends need to be invited. I always find it helpful to have a printed invitation card to give to someone. It makes the invitation a little more firm, and acts as a reminder to our guests as the event draws near. It is vital, and common courtesy, to explain to our friends as we invite them that during the evening 'so and so' will be talking briefly about 'such and such a topic' and that there will be opportunity for questions and discussion with the speaker afterwards for those who wish. It is dishonest, and hinders the work of the gospel, to get people to any event under false pretences. Try to be as natural as possible in inviting people. If you appear uptight or hesitant about inviting your friends they may be hesitant themselves about accepting, fearful of what they are letting themselves in for. And be rigorous in avoiding the use of 'Christian jargon' or over-spiritual language as you invite friends. Few non-Christians appreciate being invited to 'An evangelistic outreach' evening, or being cajoled into coming to an event 'because the Lord has really laid you upon my heart as being one whom he longs to save'!

The shape of the evening

So what shape might a typical housegroup outreach evening take!

7.30p.m. Guests begin to arrive. First impressions are important and it is vital to create a relaxed and relaxing atmosphere. The room into which people are shown should not be set out as if it were a doctor's waiting room or as if people were turning up to a church council meeting. Try to arrange chairs informally, put out bowls of crisps and nuts, have some pleasant music playing in the background. Offer people a drink when they arrive, and make them feel welcome.

7.50p.m. Serve food. This will have been set out in another room. Buffets work particularly well because they are less time-consuming than a sit-down meal and they also encourage people to circulate a little more. The meal is an important part of helping people to relax with each other. Don't try and initiate deep spiritual conversations over the meal, and warn the Christians in advance to beware of 'in' talk.

8.40p.m. Call people together and introduce the speaker. Check beforehand with the speaker how he/she would like to be introduced. I still cringe at the memory of being introduced to a group as '. . . Ian Parkinson who is an evangelist; so if he can't convert you, nobody will!' Christians who are present should not take the introduction of the speaker as a signal to pull out Bibles and/or notebooks, nor should they signify approval of points made by shouts, or even whispers, of 'Amen!', or similar. This is *not* a Christian meeting, but the opening of a home to friends and to a speaker.

The speaker should speak for no more than ten minutes. The talk should be such that discussion follows naturally. Therefore the speaker must be careful not to be so impassioned that guests are deterred from expressing any opinion which might be slightly contrary for fear of causing personal slight or offence. Do not see the talk as the only ten minutes you have to persuade a lot of unbelievers to repent. Rather, see it as facilitating a discussion through which minds and hearts might be gradually changed as guests chew over, in word and thought, the implications of the Christian message for them.

8.50p.m. The host invites comment or discussion of what has been said and offers the opportunity to question the speaker further. One group, with which I was involved, invited written questions in advance from those guests who wished to submit them. This struck me as a very good idea as it helpfully filled in any awkward gaps or silences in the proceedings, and got the question time off to a good start. The open discussion time is very important. Often it is not until many people start talking that they actually start thinking seriously through some of these issues. Loosening the tongue helps to unblock the mind!

9.20p.m. Open discussion is halted by the introduction of cups of tea and coffee. The host thanks the speaker and invites guests to talk further with the speaker personally if they have more questions to ask.

The hope is that discussion will continue, informally, in smaller groups around the room. This is the opportunity for the Christians to ask their guests for impressions of the talk and discussion, and for the speaker to move, naturally, around the different clumps of people in the room. This part of the evening is often the most valuable of all; which is why the open discussion needs to be cut short after half an hour, even when it is going strong. We need to make sure that people still have time to stick around after the open discussion has finished, rather than dash away because the hour is now late.

Any effective housegroup event will leave the group members with a good deal of follow-up. Much of this will be done on a one-to-one basis. It is often helpful to organize these events around the time of a church guest service and follow up the evening with an invitation to that service. Best of all, try to encourage those who have been helped by the housegroup event to attend a 'Just Looking' or 'Christian basics' course run by your church . . . which brings me neatly on to my final section.

Housegroups with an exclusively evangelistic purpose

In an age of great confusion and widespread ignorance about spiritual matters in general and the Christian faith in particular, most people need a good deal of practical help if they are to come to real faith in Christ. They need to have the basics of the faith carefully explained and need help in sorting out confusions and finding answers to questions. It is for this reason that many churches have, for some time, set up short-term groups for enquirers, spiritual maternity wards, if you like, where complications surrounding the new birth can be sorted out. In our own church we run 'Just Looking' courses two or three times each year. The six-week course involves simple Bible study, the use of commercially produced video material[1] and much group discussion as it tackles such topics as:

- Jesus, and why he is special
- Sin and the cross
- The resurrection: the event and its consequences
- The Holy Spirit: God's power for living
- Becoming a Christian (including the cost of commitment)
- Any questions/how to grow as a Christian.

Those who come to faith through this course are then encouraged to join a ten-week 'Foundations for Christian Living' course, which teaches basic elements of discipleship and then feeds people into our regular housegroups.

No mention of 'basics' courses would be complete without reference to two hugely effective programmes which have borne great fruit in a variety of different settings. 'Good News Down the Street' is a programme of housegroup evangelism pioneered by the Rev Michael Wooderson, a Midlands vicar[2]. Essentially, a 'Good News' team of three lay people from a local church conduct a six-week 'basics' course in the home of an 'enquirer'. Baptism, marriage, funeral and other contacts are given the opportunity of having such a team in their home, and experience has proved that there is no shortage of people willing to take up such an offer. Not only does this provide a way of mobilizing a whole church for evangelism but it also offers a wonderful opportunity for team members to develop skills and confidence in speaking of their own faith.

One of the most exciting evangelistic resources in recent years has been the development of 'Alpha', Holy Trinity, Brompton's own course in Christian basics[3]. Emerging from the rarified atmosphere of West London it has proved its ability to be used in any and every cultural and social setting with great effect. Not only are the teaching materials of the highest quality but several other features of the course contribute to its impact.

- Each evening begins with a shared meal, thus bonding the group together.
- The course includes a weekend away, although this is frequently reduced to a single Saturday away by many churches.
- It is a rolling programme. That is, each course finishes with a meal to which course members invite their own unconverted friends, and at which there is a gospel presentation and an invitation to join the next Alpha course which will shortly be commencing.

Another huge advantage of Alpha is that it is possible to buy the complete set of Alpha talks on video. Not only does this save work for hard-pressed leaders, but often in discussion groups, enquirers feel more free to disagree with a third party (i.e. the person you have both been watching on the TV) than with someone they have just heard speak directly to them in the flesh.

In the days of the New Testament church, much effective evangelism probably took place in the homes of church members. The gospel spread rapidly as existing family and social networks were used as channels along which the good news of Christ could travel. We need to recapture this vision afresh today, to see the huge possibilities for home-based evangelism and to act accordingly.

Notes

1 Useful resources include Franco Zeffirelli's *Jesus of Nazareth* (Channel 5 Video), *Journey Into Life* (Sunrise), and extracts from *Jesus Then and Now* (Lella), though this is now a little dated. CPAS have produced a video-based discussion course entitled *Christian Basics* which can be adapted for local use.

2 This is exhaustively described in *The Church Down Our Street* by Michael Wooderson (MARC Monarch Publications, 1989). A video entitled *Good News for You*, designed to help churches to use 'Good News' teams is available from The Network Trust, 100 Lazy Hill Rd., Aldridge, Walsall, WS9 8RR.

3 Full details of *Alpha* courses and materials can be obtained from The Alpha Office, Holy Trinity Brompton, Brompton Road, London, SW7 1JA (0171 581 8255). Alpha Training Conferences are regularly organized up and down the country, and a free newspaper *Alpha News* is produced several times each year.

Nick Mercer is now an Anglican curate in Northwood Hills and lives with two other church workers in Harrow, north-west London. A Cambridge graduate, he taught at Lancing College, trained for four years at Spurgeon's College and served in Baptist churches in Camberwell, Ashford, Enfield and Torquay. For ten years he was on the staff of London Bible College, lately as Assistant Principal. He hopes to return to the student world as a chaplain. He says that he has 'organized and been to more housegroups than is healthy for any human'.

I was a housegroup junkie

Nick Mercer

It's midnight and I've just got back from Richard and Dawn's. It was a fantastic housegroup. As usual I'm hyper at the moment and need to unwind before I can begin to think about sleeping. So pull up an armchair – I've got one of those special housegroup armchairs which look and feel so comfortable for the first five minutes and then begin to twist your spine as you sink into the crevice at the back. And if you try to make yourself more comfortable, one of the castors falls off (and I say, 'Oh, don't worry, it's always doing that . . .') and then you try and mend it and completely distract everybody and then you sit down and it makes a mildly rude noise which will make anyone under eighteen spend the next hour suppressing giggles. Of course, I've sprinkled milk chocolate crumbs all over the seat and these will gradually melt during the evening and work their way deeply into the fabric of your trousers. But you will be too busy trying to keep away from the traces of jam you have just discovered on the left arm to notice the chocolate. And only if you are very inquisitive will you find the unspeakable things wedged down between the seat cushion and the sides of the armchair.

So hands up if you would like a coffee. Or rather, hands up if you don't want one, or if you'd prefer tea . . . or orange. So how many coffees is that? It's special housegroup coffee, by the way. They collect all the powdery bits left in the bottom of the container ships which bring the coffee beans over from Finland (where they are used as ballast on the return trips from delivering live elks to the Highlands) and then they freeze-dry it, although you can still taste the North Sea oil a little, and certainly smell the elks, until you add the dried milk, that is. Actually it's not just any old dried milk, it's Coffeypal. That's healthier than dried milk and congeals into soft little white balls which give a whirlpool effect as you stir in the few granules of sugar which haven't stuck to the sugar spoon. It looks a little like a slightly blocked shower plug-hole.

Do help yourself to a housegroup digestive. They all have the hairline cracks which will cause them to break into a hundred pieces between the packet and your plate. It's surprising really, because biscuits that old are usually a bit softer. The silica gel I keep in the biscuit tin must help.

So shall we wait a little longer for anyone else to come, or shall we start? Let's split into small buzz groups and discuss that for just a minute or two. OK. So who would like to Open with a word of prayer? Now we'll move into a time of open sharing. I'll begin.

Just 'soft' housegroups at first

It all started when I was about fifteen, that very vulnerable age when you can fall into so many traps. I was bored with church. Sermons were beginning to lose their excitement. I couldn't ask questions and I began to realize that our minister only had two basic sermons anyway: the evangelistic 'let Jesus into your heart' sermon, and the discipleship 'pray-more, read-your-Bible-more, give-more, witness-more' sermon. On top of that, the liturgy had lost its allure and I seemed to spend most of the time working out why there were semi-colons in places where I expected commas; or adding up the hymn numbers on the board to see if they ever came to 666. Even the choruses I used to love seemed to have become devoid of intellectual challenge and kept reminding me of Barry Manilow.

Then one evening, some of my friends asked me to go to a housegroup in another church. That evening changed my life.

I knew I shouldn't really have gone. We still had a mid-week prayer meeting then, and the Prayer Warriors (Mabel and Elsie – we were very short of male Warriors – in fact we were very short of anybody) had often warned us young people, 'Just say no!' But when you're young, spiritually bored, and a born leader, and you see others going to housegroups, and it doesn't seem to make them start thinking for themselves . . . well, what harm can it do, to go just once, I thought.

But I didn't realize then how addictive housegroups were. So I had been to one meeting, and I hadn't become charismatic (another thing the Prayer Warriors had warned against), although I did get a bit of a buzz for the next day or two. Anyway, by the Sunday, I couldn't wait for Wednesday and the next meeting. It was just 'soft' housegroups at first. You know, a few choruses, a lot of 'sharing', occasionally opening the Bible and seeing how quickly we could get off the subject. 'Pooling ignorance' was what the Prayer Warriors had called it. It was great, and I couldn't get over the sense of freedom and excitement that I experienced in those heady, early days. There was Dotty Daphne, who was seriously into 'pictures', and Derek who had an uncanny knack of interpreting the most obscure 'visions'. I thought he'd be stumped by Daphne's picture of a man dressed all in black taking a white rabbit out of a top hat. But not Derek. Strangely though, we never heard back from Paul Daniels when we invited him to come and 'preach with a view'.

Of course we had to be discerning, and I well remember the theological discussion we had about the omniscience of God after Gordon gave a 'word' one week, that started 'Thus saith the Lord, "I love you my children, and have nothing against you, as far as I know . . ." ' We decided he was prophesying 'in the flesh' and he stuck to his more usual 'word' after that incident: 'Thus saith the Lord, "I love you my children and I am going to do a New Thing among you . . ." '

If those bits of Lego in the cushion are beginning to bother you, by the way, do take them out through the little tear in the cushion cover and pop them into Charles's sock which you'll find down the side of the chair there. He left it a month ago after we had laid hands on his athlete's foot at the monthly healing meeting. It didn't get any better, although Daphne's cat never had any more bowel problems after that particular prayer time.

Anyway, one thing led to another, and eventually the 'buzz' of these 'soft' housegroups began to wear off. Then I met a friend one Saturday morning in the Springs of Living Joy Christian Bookshop and Coffee House, and he told me about the housegroup run by the Strictly Particulars on Sabbath Eve at 7p.m. It had been started to try and attract young people who might otherwise be led astray by the world, the flesh and the devil on a Saturday night. (There was a jazz band playing in the Town Hall every other week.) Well, some of my friends warned me about getting into the 'hard' stuff, but before I knew where I was I had been to a meeting on Infralapsarianism and Vatican II and couldn't wait till the next Saturday when we were going to share informally on Pseudepigrapha in the Intertestamental Period. It was all downhill from there. Soon I was on Premillenarianism and the Middle East, The Significance of the Tabernacle Tent Pegs for Today, and I even led a housegroup on Predestination. I think it was 'meant'.

But after a while, just as the 'soft' had led to the 'hard' housegroups, so my search for that ever elusive Housegroup High led me to the exotic and bizarre. I am talking of the Kathmandu of 'Caring and Sharing' groups. I am talking ecumenical housegroups during Lent.

TRASH

Churches Together in Neasden (CTN) had never been very strong, mainly because it was only the Quakers, the Methodists and the 8a.m. 1662 Congregation from St Etheldredd's that attended. In fact, it was I and some friends who the following year set up CAN (Churches Apart in Neasden) and inaugurated the Truly Reformed Allcomers Summer Housegroups (TRASH) which started in March and went on till October. I was so addicted by then that even TRASHCAN failed to flash a warning light to me. The CTN groups were just week-fillers really. We used to discuss books written by Catholic abbots with sets of initials like OBJ or CSSM after their names. There were lots of long pauses and we lit candles and decided that it didn't really matter what you believed, as long as you believed it sincerely; and of course you had to be nice. I knew there was something deeply wrong with these housegroups because we didn't have coffee, we had sherry. And some of them smoked. So anyway, one week, when John, who was between churches at the time, said that all religions were basically the same, and said, 'just name any two religions you like . . . they're all the same really . . .' I said 'Christian Science and Melanesian Frog Worship.' The rest of the group thought I was very narrow-minded and Zöe pointed out that Mary Baker Eddy had kept pet frogs as a child. They didn't like the way I kept dragging the Bible into things either.

When they introduced a 'new' chorus one week – 'kum bi ya, my Lord' – I abandoned CTN as a lost cause. But it was a springboard for TRASH and soon I and a group of like-minded individuals from different churches were meeting in house-groups almost every evening. I didn't realize it then, but in reality I was getting TRASHED every night.

If you want to use my housegroup 'bathroom' by the way, it's at the top of the stairs. You can't miss it, and if you do, you will stumble into a room with resentful-looking teenagers in it, with earphones on, who will give you a 'just you dare try and have an I'm-really-interested-in-young-people conversation, and we'll smoke our pot in front of you and see if you tell our parents' sneer. The light switch for the bathroom is in the airing cupboard. The obvious switch outside the bathroom door will turn the living room lights out, so we know when to laugh and shout up to you where the switch is. And I think you'll find that the key in the bathroom door doesn't quite turn. But it does make a lot of noise, and if you should manage to turn it, you will only be able to unlock it by putting your shoulder under the door handle and forcing the whole door up on its hinges. Someone will probably have to shout those instructions through the bathroom door to you while we're saying the grace together. There's a knack to flushing the loo. If you don't catch it with another twist of the handle just a second after the initial turn, then you have to wait for the cistern to fill again. It's a very slow filler, so probably I'll send someone up to shout through the door, 'Are you alright?'

As you can imagine, trying to support a habit like TRASH was very expensive and demanding. In the end, I even sold my guitar to pay for coffee and digestives. I knew I was out of control when I sent out a prayer letter to friends 'looking to the Lord for support for my Neasden-wide ministry . . .' But it wasn't just the financial burden, it was the demands on my imagination and the group's own giftings that led to my ultimate demise. Here's a typical evening.

Arrive at 7p.m. for 8.30p.m.
Coffee and digestives
Move into a time of open notices
Welcome latecomers
Discuss who should open in prayer
Welcome latecomers
Sing choruses (Tricky without the guitar, but fortunately Donna had a real gift for the gazoo, and she was only sixteen. Later we were to discover the freedom of Kendrick Karaoke tapes.)
Alan leads the next in his 15-week series on 'Skin Diseases in Leviticus'. (We all assure him that his face is looking a lot better now and that seventeen *is* a difficult age.)
Joyce arrives and apologizes for her lateness (she does this every week). (She had a divine appointment with a man on the 39 bus whose dog had just died and who had been

wondering about re-incarnation. She was able to share with him everything that Donald had told us the week before about Ecclesiastes and Tibetan Tantric practice. He had been very interested and said he would give Buddhism serious consideration. Doesn't God work in mysterious ways?)

Alan says he has to go home because he has no lights on his bike. (Although I notice that Neasden Wanderers are on *Match of the Day*.)

Move into a time of open prayer. (We focus on Alan's face and the man on the 39 bus. Jeanette isn't here tonight so we skip praying for her aunt's bunions just this one week.)

Discuss who should close in prayer.

Coffee and digestives. (Chocolate digestives if it was someone's birthday, and it usually was.)

Continue fellowshipping informally with a Summer Ripeness Worship Cassette in the background.

'I desperately needed help'

Of course, not every evening was as exciting as this. But I think this gives you a tantalizing flavour of what housegroups can be like. I've not gone into too much salacious detail as you might end up being drawn into my spiral of housegroup degradation. (Although I can't help mentioning the inverted catering pyramid. Each week, the host and hostess try to present a more lavish and yet 'casual' spread of refreshments than the people who catered the previous week. So you start with the traditional coffee and digestives and three months later you're snacking on venison vol-au-vents, crème brûlée tarts and non-alcoholic pina colada.)

I only understood the true extent of my dependency when one memorable evening the meeting was at my place, and nobody turned up. (I was so out of touch and had 'lost it' to such a degree that I had not even realized that Neasden Wanderers were in a Cup replay at home.) I found myself saying to Trevor McDonald at the end of *News At Ten* 'thank you for sharing that.' I was shaking and in a cold sweat. When I asked the continuity announcer to close in prayer after the National Anthem, she didn't, and I knew I had become that Housegroup Junkie I had always despised. I desperately needed help.

The Prayer Warriors, Elsie and Mabel, unknown to me, had been praying for me all this time. They had a friend, Arthur Pastey, who founded Capernaum Re-Roofing Ministries (remember that disastrous housegroup in Mark 2?). He ran a self-help meeting for housegroup junkies at Gadarene Grange. It was very informal and really just a time for open sharing with other addicts. But there was one big difference. We had to completely ignore one another. You'd sit there and say things like 'I'd just like to share how I'm feeling . . .' and no-one would look at you. Or Arthur would say, 'And what do you think of that, Linda?' and Linda would have to keep polishing her nails. There was no coffee or digestives and Arthur would deliberately not close in prayer. We had Pastor Pastey's telephone number and could ring him at any time of the evening if we felt a housegroup coming on.

Of course, they say you're never really cured. I still kept saying 'really' and 'just' and I had to keep out of any groups in homes involving six people or more, otherwise I started sharing uncontrollably. I used to miss the closeness and warmth that the housegroup gave, but I discovered that rush-hour on the Northern Line seemed to meet those needs. Last month my nephew had a gazoo for his birthday, and I found myself involuntarily closing my eyes and lifting up my head with a beatific smile, hands aloft, as he played 'Old McDonald had a Farm'.

Now I know what you're thinking. You're wondering why I was at Richard and Dawn's housegroup tonight. Well, we had an itinerant evangelist in town last week leading a Neasden-wide Name It And Claim It Celebration. When he said there was a man in the tent with a secret sin that involved other people, I just really knew he was speaking to me. I went forward, had a spirit of Small Congregations cast out of me by one of the ministry team (Daphne, actually) and I've never looked back since. (That's because I hurt my neck as I fell over.) I was spectacularly healed of my addiction.

Would anyone like to close in prayer?

P.S

So you have got to the end and you are still alive! We hope you found the chapters of this book stimulating, challenging and above all filled with practical help for getting the best out of your housegroup.

Congratulations on hanging in there as a small-group leader! You are often in a position of being taken for granted, and we are sure there are days when you wonder if God has called together all the most difficult people in your church and put them in your housegroup, just to keep you humble.

Despite all these tensions, God continues to use small groups to help people come to faith and to grow in their faith. Thousands of Christians in Britain today receive most of their pastoral support, encouragement and opportunity to develop their gifts in the context of a group like yours. So be encouraged. You are not alone, and the work you put in week by week is time invested, not wasted!

Now that you have read this Survival Guide you may feel a little overwhelmed at trying to digest all the information. It is probably best just to try and put into practice one or two ideas at a time. Give yourself and your group enough space to cope with the changes. Remember that not everyone handles change very well and it may take the group some time to get up to speed with your enthusiasm for a particular change.

In addition to the people skills, it is very difficult to develop the Bible skills which you need. It is worth getting hold of a Bible concordance and a one-volume Bible commentary.

To help get to grips with the Bible, the *Crossway Bible Guides* were written with this specific purpose in mind. These guides are not intended to make you look cleverer than you are (although they will probably do that!), but they are intended to give you a clear grasp of the text so that the whole group can encounter the Bible in a meaningful way. They should provide an excellent resource to enable you to make sure you are using the Bible correctly and to help everyone begin to apply the Bible to their lives. More and more books of the Bible are being covered, and some lesser-known Old Testament books will prove stimulating and helpful as you use this series.

We cannot emphasize strongly enough how your leadership of the group must come in the context of your own growth in faith. When you prepare next week's study, set about it not just with the primary aim of getting some good discussion questions for the group. Approach the Bible with a hungry heart, praying for God to speak to *you* through Scripture. Once truth has gripped you, it is likely that God will enable you to grip others with it too. The best leaders are those who are excited by their subject.

You have a special calling in leading your housegroup. May God grant you joy in your leadership of those men and women God has given into your care. Our prayer is that as the Bible becomes alive to you, so your group will be increasingly made alive through the Word of God.

Making the Bible come alive

This book has been written to help busy housegroup leaders. Among the many challenges faced in leading a small group week by week is the need to keep the Bible study fresh and relevant.

The *Crossway Bible Guides* have been written with this challenge in mind. The series can be used for either personal or group study. The guides have been written by people who have a proven track record in teaching the Bible and each book breaks up the passage into manageable sections.

There are several key features designed to help housegroup leaders.

- Each section includes discussion questions which are an ideal starter for discussion in a housegroup.
- The essential meaning of each passage is dealt with in non-technical language.
- Important themes are dealt with in brief, readable summaries.
- Each *Crossway Bible Guide* divides the text in a way that enables it to be studied by a group over a number of weeks.
- The books cover both Old and New Testaments, providing a balanced approach to Bible study.
- The 'user-friendly' style and layout make them easy to work with.
- The series will eventually build to cover every book of the Bible, providing a complete set of volumes.

The *Crossway Bible Guides* began appearing in 1993 and have steadily grown in popularity, in proving useful for personal study as well as a teaching aid for housegroups.

If you are looking for reliable, readable and reasonably priced books to help bring Bible study alive in your housegroup, the titles currently available in the *Crossway Bible Guide* series are listed below.

Series Editors	Ian Coffey
	Stephen Gaukroger
Old Testament Editor	Stephen Dray
New Testament Editor	Stephen Motyer

Exodus **Stephen Dray**

Through this invaluable study guide we discover that Exodus still speaks to us today. We see that we face many of the same trials and dilemmas and that God helps his peope still.

Leviticus **Derek Tidball**

Leviticus contains a dazzling collection of gems of truth, embedded in the God-centred society of old Israel. Mined, polished and displayed by an expert, their lustre is as appropriate for our own culture as it was in their original Old Testament setting.

Joshua **Charles Price**

Joshua is a book about God! He is revealed as a God of action in the cut and thrust of life. From Joshua we learn not only that God is indispensable; he is available to those who are available to him and follow him.

Ezra &
Nehemiah **Dave Cave**

These books are powerful examples of God's care for his people. His equipping of leaders for his people is as vital and dynamic as in Old Testament times.

Psalms 1–72 **Alan Palmer**

Psalms have formed the backbone of Christian worship. Discussion questions and background information to each psalm bring these wonderful hymns to life – to our modern life today. We experience with the psalmists a wide range of emotions and are led into a direct relationship with God.

Isaiah **Philip Hacking**

Isaiah wrote to rulers and to people from all walks of life. Centuries have passed but conditions and attitudes are often strikingly similar today. These studies in Isaiah help us to focus on the essentials of daily living in the light of a sure bright hope for tomorrow.

Haggai, Zechariah and Malachi **John James**

The three prophets who had returned from exile each brought a powerful message and were instrumental in rebuilding the spiritual fortunes of God's people. With Haggai we learn how to rebuild our lives, Zechariah reveals the power of God over all the nations of the earth; and Malachi calls us to abandon dry and meaningless ritual and to worship God from the heart.

Mark **David Hewitt**

The gospel of Mark vividly describes the life, death and resurrection of Jesus as Son of God. It encourages his readers to believe in Jesus and to act on that belief, equipping persecuted and threatened churches with hope in the context of stark reality.

Acts **Stephen Gaukroger**

Acts is one of the most exciting and relevant Bible books for Christians today. It shows us God powerfully at work in the early church.

1 Corinthians **Robin Dowling and Stephen Dray**

Paul calls the Christians at Corinth to unite against the pressures of pagan life which threaten to engulf them. Here is teaching, sharply relevant to our own day, on:

- Marriage and singleness; consicence and compromise,
- The Lord's Supper; the conduct of worship,
- The gifts of the Holy Spirit, and
- Love, the power of the resurrection.

Ephesians **Steve Motyer**

Paul urges the Ephesian church to be at one; to be a place:

- of strength for spirutual warfare,
- where relationships are transformed by God's grace, and peace,
- where wholeness of living is vibrantly expressed.

Philippians **Ian Coffey**

In his letter to the Philippians Paul writes about the reality and fullness of living as the people of God.

- He motivates us towards personal holiness,
- demonstrates life as it should be in our local church and
- directs us to a Christ-like servant relationship to others.

Timothy and Titus **Michael Griffiths**

Through these letters we are transported to ancient Ephesus and Crete where we find situations painfully similar to our own: false teaching splitting the churches, untrained and inadequate leaders, men arguing with women about their place in church life, love of money and status. Paul's letters of encouragement give us a pattern of hope for the restoration of spiritual truth and good order in our churches.

1 Peter **Andrew Whitman**

The apostle Peter encourages us to have hope in all circumstances because God's love for us is sure, he is always in control and God is in charge of the future.

Other volumes in the series will be published over the next few years, including:

1 Samuel: **Geoff Lucas**

Minor prophets: **Michael Wilcock**

John's Gospel: **Ian Barclay**